The Handbook of Ordinary Heroes

Lama Jigme Rinpoche

## Other Works by this Author

*A Path of Wisdom*, Rabsel Éditions, 2012
*Working with Emotions*, Rabsel Publications, 2019

# The Handbook of Ordinary Heroes
## Lama Jigme Rinpoche

Structure and Formatting by Audrey Desserrières.
Translated from the French by Jourdie Ross.

**RABSEL**
PUBLICATIONS

Special thanks from the translator to Audrey Desserrières, Arnaud Duhayon, Cédric Georges, Taylor Ross, Michael Ross, and Seth Watkins.

RABSEL PUBLICATIONS
16, rue de Babylone
76430 La Remuée, France
www.rabsel.com
contact@rabsel.com

This project was supported by the DRAC and Normandy Region under the FADEL Normandie, France.

© Rabsel Publications, La Remuée, France, 2016, 2019
ISBN 979-10-93883-10-6

# Table of Contents

# Introduction

Is Buddhism a religion or a philosophy? Such is the perpetual question of journalists and of the curious. The greatest Eastern masters, modern philosophers, and renowned academics have all contributed to this debate.

This is not the place to argue in favor of one theory or another. It seems reasonable to say that Buddhism is a religion for those who practice it as such, just as it is a philosophy for those who consider it exclusively based on this perspective. The proposition of this book is to approach Buddhism from another angle. Here, we consider the original purpose for the Buddha's teaching: to offer a method for how to be and how to act—in other words, how to live our humanity while taking care of ourselves and others.

The Buddha was born in India more than 2,500 years ago. His teachings later spread throughout all of Asia. The cultures of India, Tibet, China, Japan, and Thailand have little in common despite all being located in the East. And yet, each of these countries has fully integrated the Buddha's teaching, along with many other nations beyond this list. In each case, the assimilation took time, several centuries in the case of Tibet, despite its close proximity to India.

From the East, the Buddha's teaching arrived in the West in the midst of the identity crisis of the 1970s. Europe and the United States welcomed the Buddha's message, and also the folklore that came with it. As a result, the first aspiring meditators had serious work to do to separate the exotic cultural aspect from the message in order to understand the teaching and apply it.

Becoming Buddhist does not mean adopting a particular lifestyle, dressing a certain way, or stringing multiple rosaries around one's neck. Above all, it means questioning our way of conceiving and perceiving the world. This introspection allows us to become aware of our habits and our flaws. By guiding this process, the Buddha's teaching constitutes a handbook that allows us to progress toward greater freedom in order to access our innate qualities.

Discovering different cultures is interesting and enriching, but this is not the goal of the Buddhist teaching. The Buddha shared his discovery with the wish that his experience would be useful to others. His message invites us to get to know ourselves: to observe the concepts, ideas, and feelings that we experience and to understand how they color our perceptions and orient our acts—acts for which we must take responsibility and the consequences of which we will necessarily face.

Buddhism is said to be universal because it transcends all notions of time and culture. A shepherd from the

Middle Ages can apply it just as easily as a businessman from the 21st century. That said, the integration of the teaching cannot be solely intellectual. Though knowledge and know-how together constitute an important step, they are not an end in-and-of themselves. If this were the case, Buddhism would simply be a dogma of rules to follow with no individual responsibility. The Buddha's teaching has no other purpose than its personal application, whatever the nature of the individual, his[1] lifestyle or his age. This path of wisdom begins with a simple observation: all beings wish for happiness and no one wants to suffer. Based on this observation, Shakyamuni Buddha[2] set out on a quest for lasting happiness—one not subject to alteration through time or change. To attain this objective, he initially identified the causes that prevent us from being happy so that we can act upon them.

The breadth of teachings across the various cultures that have integrated Buddhism developed based on this initial quest and discovery and continue to be transmitted today. This book originated from a series of seminars taught at Dhagpo Kagyu Ling, in Dordogne, France, between 2006 and 2015, conceived based on the text of Tibetan master Gyelse Togme Zangpo, *The Thirty Seven-Fold Practice of a Bodhisattva*[3].

---

1   Translator's note: In French, pronouns take the gender of the word they refer to. For example, "someone" becomes "he" while "a person" becomes "she." In this translation, I chose to use the male pronoun "he" throughout for the purposes of simplicity. It does not reflect a gender bias on the part of the author, nor the translator.

2   The historical Buddha Siddartha Gautama, who lived sometime between the sixth and fourth centuries BCE.

3   *The Thirty Seven-Fold Practice of a Bodhisattva*, Gyelse Togme, Éditions Padmakara, Plazac, France, 2006.

The author composed this text in the fourteenth century. He wrote in verse for ease of memorization, a widely-adopted practice in the Buddhist tradition. As students frequently learned texts by heart, the composition of texts respects precise formal constraints such as metric rhythm and versification. These "root texts" are thus often quite concise and can prove relatively difficult to decipher for novices. In Tibet, such works are typically accompanied by complementary explanations, called commentaries or exegeses, which provide additional details and clarify the meaning of the root text. The student memorizes the root text and retains this memory as a reminder of the vaster meaning studied.

*The Thirty Seven-Fold Practice of a Bodhisattva* constitutes the concise and precise root text written in verse. All Tibetan students know this work by heart. Though its composition is close to vernacular, further explanations remain useful to understand it properly. The purpose of this book is not to present a new translation of the text, already widely translated elsewhere, but to deliver its message and essence so that it may be useful to Europeans and Americans today, more than seven hundred years after its composition.

Trying to literally apply the words of a fourteenth century master to our daily lives as men and women of the twenty-first century might seem a bit farfetched and only minimally useful. The point is rather to understand the meaning and to integrate it into our own culture and context. Therefore, this book does not include the stanzas of the root text accompanied with a commentary. Instead, the book presents the instructions in chapter form to make the meaning accessible to the interested reader so that he can make use of it as a practical guide.

In the original text, Gyelse Togme Zangpo describes the state of mind and daily approach for acting as a bodhisattva in thirty-seven points. What is a bodhisattva? At the start, a bodhisattva is an ordinary being who develops his understanding and application of enlightened mind over time—enlightened mind being the profound wish that all beings meet with lasting happiness and experience protection from all causes for unhappiness or any form of dissatisfaction. In other words, enlightened mind is kindness and compassion.

A bodhisattva is thus a clear-minded person who is instantly aware of each thought as it manifests without being bothered by the emotions that may color his thoughts. The cognitive or emotional occurrences that may arise are no longer a source of confusion or miscomprehension. On the contrary, such a being is able to discern all of the causes that give rise to a particular reaction.

Gyelse Togme Zangpo carried out a great deal of research in order to discover how bodhisattvas live, the nature of their state of mind, and how they act in every possible circumstance. He then summarized his findings into thirty-seven essential points. Reading this text gives the impression that living as a bodhisattva is a great challenge. The final result, as described in the original verses, might seem out of our reach. However, it is important not to become discouraged and to keep in mind the fact that we simply need to progress at our own rhythm in order to achieve our goal. After all, all bodhisattvas started out as ordinary beings, just like us.

The Buddhist teaching of the Great Vehicle offers a concrete method to progressively develop as individuals in order to face the challenges of everyday life in a new way. Generally speaking, we find solutions to our problems. However, we may notice that these solutions often prove quite temporary; the problem is resolved for several hours, days, or months, but in the end the same situation reappears and we realize that we are going in circles. Obviously, it is not possible to apply the lifestyle of a bodhisattva to a "T," but we can begin with what is in our reach. We can become more familiar with this path based on regular practical application. We will acquire a progressively more correct understanding and thus develop and obtain long-term results. Even if we do not manage to resolve a given problem today, having knowledge of the teaching and relating it to our current circumstances offers another perspective on the situation. This alternative perspective is useful for the present moment as well as for the future.

The practice of bodhisattvas can be broken down into a series of fairly simple exercises that directly connect with our daily lives. What do we encounter day after day? Outer circumstances and inner experiences that often take us from tears to laughter, and from depression to euphoria to plain indifference. The goal of this book is to give us the keys to approach our daily lives based on the values of enlightened mind: kindness and compassion.

We often read books in one sitting; we understand them relatively literally and we come away from them with new information, but we do not carry them with us into our daily lives. Here, we are concerned with seeing our emotions, our problems, our joys—all of the experiences that we encounter—and bringing them to the path of the bodhisattva by asking ourselves, "What would a bodhisattva do in my situation?" This is how we allow these ideas to permeate our minds and thus become familiar with this path in order to make it our own.

In the beginning, the advice might seem strange and foreign because it is counterintuitive to our habitual functioning. As we start off on the path, we must first become familiar with and understand this habitual functioning and see that it is similar for all human beings. Based on this foundation, it becomes natural to put effort into following the bodhisattva's path. One must also be aware that it is possible to apply the teaching artificially, to enact it without understanding its meaning. We can even develop the habit of acting as the teaching describes, but in the end we do not truly understand why we are acting in this way. This approach does not work in the long-term and does not bring results. Natural practical application signifies that we have first understood the meaning of the instruction, and, based on this understanding, our conduct occurs spontaneously rather than based on obligation or a forced attitude.

In particular, this teaching helps us understand how to communicate with and understand others. It presents an alternative way to reflect and to resolve problems and difficulties, all while genuinely helping others when the opportunity presents itself.

I would also like to invite the reader to revisit and question what he understands of the terms used here, so as not to fall captive to a first impression of his reading. The terms are intentionally simple in order to transmit the meaning, but simple does not mean simplistic. The

Buddha's teaching always gives the impression of being easy to understand, but as soon as we begin to question the meaning of the words, we can see that coming up with precise definitions is difficult. However, the explanations, such as those of *The Practice of Bodhisattvas in Thirty-Seven Stances*, are clear. By remaining as close as possible to the meaning, we can observe that the teaching does not prove as complex as it appears. Repeatedly coming back to the various subjects covered allows us to understand them with greater and greater depth. Carrying out this exercise allows us to develop clarity of mind—an understanding that goes beyond the superficial grasp of the words read. Study and contemplation constitute an important practice on the Buddhist path; they allow us to develop the clarity of mind that is useful for concrete application of the teaching in daily life. Because we study the meaning and develop our understanding beforehand, application occurs more naturally.

While intellectual understanding is undeniably an ingredient, it is not, however, an end in itself. Indeed, this comprehension is not yet complete and is influenced by our opinions and our habitual thinking. We cannot fully integrate the meaning of the teaching based on intellect alone. Therefore, we employ another practice: meditation. Meditation allows us to pacify the mind and thus introduce a new habit. If the mind remains in a calm state, it becomes much more peaceful. If we practice meditation regularly, this relaxed mind becomes a habit. Though one cannot see it from the outside, the mind itself is free from tension. A calm mind has a greater capacity for understanding.

The meditation in question here—and which we will come back to in greater detail—is a Buddhist practice.

Similar to yoga, meditation has become associated with various practices of relaxation and mindfulness. These methods function very well and easily allow one to achieve the desired goal: relative comfort and well-being, like taking an aspirin to relieve a headache without acting upon the initial cause of the headache. In the Buddhist context, the goal of meditation is not simply relaxation or well-being, but rather the development of the capacities of our mind: its clarity and discernment. Achieving this objective requires hard work and effort; otherwise our habits quickly take over. Meditation as a form of relaxation or stress-relief is one thing, but meditating to truly develop discernment and clarity of mind is another.

Furthermore, we must add a third practice to those of study and meditation: application in daily life. Without the combination of these three aspects, we cannot achieve veritable progress on the path. Applying the teaching does not mean forcing oneself to think in a certain way. The teaching is information that we receive. We then try to put in place the methods that it proposes. This application allows us to better understand the message we have received. It consists of a gradual change in our hearing. It is a reference that we can come back to, like that of the conduct and state of mind of a bodhisattva, which serve as example and inspiration. The teachings are not rules we have to follow. We always have a choice. The Buddha himself called on us to acquire our own experience, to put his teachings to the test and verify them for ourselves.

The goal of Buddhist practice is to orient ourselves in the direction that yields freedom from unhappiness and suffering in order to achieve a state free from all dissatisfaction. For this, it is necessary to maintain a given direction in one's life in order to develop on the path. Even if we strive for perfection, we cannot be perfect at every moment or act in a purely beneficial manner. The directions to follow proposed here are those of enlightened mind, of kindness and compassion toward all beings. The concept is noble and seductive. But when we commit to this path, we are sure to meet with difficulties connected to our functioning and our habits. Truly being a bodhisattva is difficult, but we can advance at our own rhythm, as it is an ongoing process. The teachings advise us not to become discouraged or to try to go too fast. On the contrary, they instruct us to evolve concretely in accordance with our capacities, by testing our application in daily life. In this way, our pursuit of progress on the path is fueled by a habit anchored within us that allows us to advance from where we are to the attainment of the final goal.

Following the path of enlightened mind means living a meaningful life while being useful to others. If this is the direction we wish to pursue, our thoughts and daily acts are an ideal training ground for progress. In the same way that it is necessary to exercise regularly to get into good physical condition, we must train our minds daily to become bodhisattvas. On an individual level, we try to develop and to progress by adjusting our attitude. This occurs on the basis of awareness; we identify our mistakes and the places where we can do better and, in this way, progress. Our attitude and our vision of others changes completely. Our way of dealing with the emotional and conceptual occurrences that influence us and the different habits related to our cultural context changes as well. This allows us to deal with difficulties much more peacefully and to act in a more beneficial way. As a result, the consequences of our acts are also more positive.

According to the Buddha's teaching, this life is not the limit of our existence. Death and rebirth continually succeed each other. However, our way of thinking is limited to the scale of a single lifetime. Most of us assume that we are born and then exist up until the moment of our death. It is therefore important to us not to live in miserable conditions, to get a good education, to achieve financial stability, etc. The Buddha's teaching includes these aspects but does not limit itself to this perspective. The teachings take our successive lifetimes into account, and this approach influences the conception of existence and progress on the path.

Karma is another fundamental Buddhist notion. It is the mechanism of causes and their consequences. Without a profound understanding of this mechanism, we always think that what we experience depends on something or someone else when, in fact, what we experience depends on us. A question arises here: how do we create positive conditions? By acquiring greater awareness of our thoughts, our words, and our actions, we can then take care of ourselves. This is the proposition of the bodhisattva's practice: master your mind; be of benefit to all; do not harm others.

Even if the example of the daily lives of bodhisattvas does not change us from one day to the next, it does, however, constitute a solid, information-rich basis for reflection. We can implement simple things according to our capacities and our environment. In this way, we come closer to the ideal of the bodhisattva step by step.

Dipping into the experience of everyday life and our interactions with others is fertile ground for acquiring a better understanding of our functioning and also that of others. The majority of human beings go through numerous problems and difficulties due to their emotions, as well as all of the concepts that they cultivate. Life is in perpetual movement; nothing is immutable and everything inevitably changes. The temporary nature of existence and of all things is a source of dissatisfaction and unhappiness. Once satisfied, our expectations and desires give way to new expectations and desires. All human beings live according to this same basic functioning. When the mind is less caught up in its own narrative and more attentive to others, we more clearly perceive the situations in which we find ourselves. Our way of relating to others becomes more beneficial—less colored by judgment—as attachment to our feelings perturbs us less strongly. We experience greater kindness and compassion. A change takes place in our minds; we understand what is happening and others' reactions better. Life becomes simpler, more pleasant, and more useful as well. The mind is more relaxed and more open to the situations that it encounters, and thus, we have greater freedom.

If this training remains purely intellectual, it will not yield results. Instead, we acquire a form of knowledge that we cannot put to concrete use. For example, we all know that a car has a motor, but if our car were to break down on the highway, we would be powerless because we do not know how to fix it. Staying on the intellectual level alone comes down to the same thing: all of the knowledge accumulated will be of no use to us in concrete circumstances. Kindness and compassion are not notions to acquire, but qualities to embody with sincerity. When we do this, all of our experiences, all of our perceptions, become working material that we can use. The practice of Buddhism is no longer limited to our meditation cushion. Every aspect of life becomes an authentic practice.

I would like to specify one thing. In the course of my forty years teaching in the West, I have realized that certain people think that suffering—from one kind of pain or another—is a good thing because it concerns rightful punishment or allows one to "purify negative acts." This is a misunderstanding of the Buddha's teaching. We do not need to suffer to be bodhisattvas. Unhappiness simply constitutes the result of a negative act carried out in the past, neither purification nor punishment. The teachings give solutions to sustainably remedy this unhappiness by identifying its causes to avoid reproducing them.

The bodhisattva's path allows for the development of another vision, a different comprehension of what we experience and the situations that we encounter, which thus allows us to live in greater harmony with ourselves and others.

Chapter 1

# The State of Affairs

Following the path of the bodhisattva begins by ascertaining the state of affairs of our existence, similar to the image of walking into a new apartment. The more carefully we consider this state of affairs, the fewer surprises we will run into later! Leaving out this step can easily lead to playing a role or pretending. Like an actor, the practitioner takes up a style, as it were, and thus considers that he has started on the path of the bodhisattva; in fact, he is doing nothing more than acting out a role. Generally speaking, such an approach to the path reaches its conclusion fairly quickly. This is why the Buddhist path begins with an observation: what is happening within us? The true beginning of the bodhisattva's path means turning our gaze inward, toward the mind. How are ideas, thoughts, and concepts born? What defines us? As we begin, the goal consists of observing what happens within us and taking note of the elements that trigger an emotion, their repercussions on our acts, and the consequences that unfold from this. In this way, we become more aware of our own functioning.

It is not necessary to force yourself to take a certain direction; the idea is to adopt a new point of view. This simple practice already orients our lives in a different way. As such, the way we use our time, and even the way we act, changes.

In general, the difficulty lies in our habits; we have a tendency to go along with what happens in life without taking the time to observe or reflect. Situations, just like thoughts, unfold one after another, practically without space for breath, nor perspective to try and understand them. And yet, perspective—space—often generates another kind of comprehension of the value of life.

Thus, the bodhisattva's path begins by becoming aware of what is: our body, our mind, our way of functioning, and the temporary, transitory conditions that make up our lives and our being.

## Body and Mind

We can begin our reflection with human existence. We are endowed with a human body. The Buddha qualified this existence as "precious" and invited us to reflect on this. Understanding the importance of human existence allows for clarification of the direction we wish to take in life.

As human beings, we adhere to certain concepts inherent to this condition. For each of us, life begins at birth, lasts a certain amount of time, and concludes with death. All of our knowledge is based on and influenced by others: parents, education, society, cultural customs and mores, etc. The majority of people think that a good education gives us access to a job and professional life sufficient to sustain our family and lead a happy life. The image here is intentionally stereotypical to emphasize the process.

Consider adult life, more specifically. Once you have finished school, the process of establishing your adult life begins. Perhaps ten, fifteen, or twenty years are necessary to accomplish what we wish—get married, have kids, acquire possessions, and enjoy our good professional and social position (according to an ideal scenario). A few decades later, it's already time to give up, little by little, all that we have constructed because we are in physical and mental decline. Retirement comes fast, as our faculties are not as sharp as they once were and we are losing energy. This is everyone's lot. Like the inhabitants of a buzzing anthill, we occupy ourselves preparing a life we barely have time to enjoy. Do we truly realize the brevity of this life?

The Buddha invites us to appreciate this human existence because it is ephemeral, for one, but also because we are endowed with precious capabilities. Normally, we do not make much of what is intrinsic to our very being. We rarely think of ordinary life as precious, and yet this life is an extraordinary vehicle with great potential for development and progress. Human beings can rejoice in this, all while taking care not to waste this precious opportunity.

To attain a good understanding of this potential, it is necessary to take another look at the habitual functioning of all human beings. We all want to become someone and accomplish something. We invest time and energy in attaining our goals and satisfying our desires. With a little luck, we do not commit harmful acts on the way, but this is not always the case. We often find it necessary to cheat the odds a little and find ways to bias outcomes in our favor. Often enough, we achieve success based on outdoing or undermining our competition. I am not talking about con artistry or fraud, but simply a state of mind reflected in our acts to achieve our own ends. Often, we do not even notice this state of mind. We are so focused on the goal we wish to achieve that we do not see the harmful acts we commit in order to succeed. In this context, the term "harmful" means "not in harmony with the bodhisattva's path." We do not truly understand the functioning of karma—the fact that a cause brings about a consequence of identical nature. By being solely focused on the end result, we do not pay attention to the acts we commit and we fool ourselves into believing in the success of the moment, without seeing any further. We do not realize that we will experience the consequences that our acts engender at a given moment. The Buddha used the term "ignorance" to designate this state of mind. In the Buddhist context, ignorance does not refer to a kind of stupidity, but rather to the fact of not recognizing what is truly happening and being carried away by the feeling of the moment.

Our project thus concerns attentive analysis of our situation and reflection on what the terms "illusion" and "ignorance" signify. Correct understanding of these two ideas opens a new door. Negative acts can have positive results in the immediate future. However, due to the natural mechanism of karma, a result will always manifest in correlation with the cause generated. Although it is difficult for us to connect each consequence we experience with its initial cause, the mechanism of karma is an ineluctable process.

Based on the society in which we live, we currently have an idea of what we need to accomplish as well as the means to do so. But if we step back and observe our minds and what is happening within them with greater awareness of our acts and attitudes, a wish to live in a different way emerges. This does not mean making radical decisions or implementing drastic changes, but simply acquiring a quality of awareness that begins with an observation of our present situation: our minds and conditions as human beings.

Our individual experiences constitute the basis for progress. Little by little, we see the areas where we need to pay attention and we sort out our priorities in accordance with this. This awareness begins with the realization that human existence is precious. Based on the understanding of the value of this life, it becomes possible to put it to good use without wasting time.

Human existence has value because it constitutes an opportunity to free oneself from all unhappiness. Our current living conditions are an amalgam of happiness and suffering. Despite our profound wish to encounter pleasant conditions, we expend great energy to achieve conditions that are nevertheless temporary and we continue to be battered by waves of varying intensities of satisfaction followed by dissatisfaction, like a boat on a stormy sea. However, thanks to this existence, it is possible to evolve beyond these fluctuations.

An intellectual understanding remains different from a more profound perception, a personal experience. It is as though a dense fog envelops our minds and we do not truly manage to integrate the meaning. However, a more profound perception can be the impetus for change. The absence of this perception is why the Buddha's teaching often sounds to us like a pretty myth that we will never personally achieve. The primary problem is that we do not perceive our current conditions, nor the functioning of our minds. Obscuration is not a black wall standing before us; it is simply the fact that we hear and know things without having a personal experience of them.

The same is true of human existence. We are intellectually aware of its value, but we do not profoundly integrate this awareness. Due to this, we are always carried away by our perception of the moment without succeeding in getting a wider perspective. Our life unfolds this way. We follow what arises within us, moment after moment, like a leaf pushed first one way and then another by the wind.

Buddhist masters, notably Gampopa (1079–1153 CE[4]), insist upon this idea and on that of human existence because they have clearly seen the process that leads to its acquisition. The Buddha explained that the death of the physical body does not constitute an end, for the mind continues and reincarnates in a new matrix. Migrating from one life to another is a process subject to conditions. The Buddha's teaching indicates the existence of six different types of destinies or forms of existence. As a human being, we can directly perceive two of these: the destinies of human and animal life. The others are beyond our field of perception for the moment, but the

---

4    See *The Jewel Ornament of Liberation*: The Wish-fulfilling Gem of the Noble Teachings, Gampopa, Snow Lion Publications, Ithaca, New York, 1998.

Buddha clearly perceived and described them[5]. Within these different destinies, there are categories. For example, there are different types of animal species.

We are born human, but what happens when this existence comes to term? At the end of this life, we have the possibility of being reborn among one of the six destinies. The consciousness—or mind—connects to a possibility, that is, a physical body, which develops, is born, lives, and dies. Among humans, the consciousness penetrates a new matrix through the parents. Consciousness is not human form. The parents create the physical container of the human body, and this body constitutes a possibility to which consciousness connects. The human being then keeps this destiny until death.

Mind has no form; it is clear awareness that connects to a form. In the case of a human destiny, the body offers a possibility to act and accomplish things. The body is thus a vehicle. A car allows one to go quickly from point A to point B. However, the vehicle and the passenger are distinct from one another. The same is true for the consciousness and the body. When the human body no longer functions because the conditions for its good working order are no longer united, it dies. The consciousness naturally directs itself toward a new opportunity. Having found one, it then incarnates and lives according to its new existence. This is how the mind connects with different types of life.

The question that arises is this: On what basis do we obtain a new life form? Everyone is endowed with consciousness. Why do we not choose the best option for life? Everything depends on what we have prepared. No

---

5    See *The Jewel Ornament of Liberation* for more on the six destinies.

one decides our destination. The unification of diverse causes and circumstances offers the possibility to connect with a new opportunity for life. If a seed is planted in fertile soil and it receives all the necessary elements for its proper development, the plant will grow. However, the same seed simply placed in water will not be able to grow in the same way. A different soil, rich in other nutrients, will yield yet another type of growth.

All beings are reborn based on their respective karma, that is, according to the nature—beneficial, neutral, or harmful—of the acts that they have committed during their existence. After death, karma conditions the new birth, whether it be human, animal, or otherwise. Whatever the destiny, the same inexorable process applies: a being is born, undergoes various experiences, dies, is born again, undergoes yet other experiences, dies anew, and so on. This cycle engenders a great deal of agitation. Indeed, we act in every moment and every act, of thought, speech, or physical body, sows a karmic seed that will have an effect. The sum of these consequences produces a given type of life. Some are more pleasant; others, in contrast, prove more difficult, colored by suffering. Most are a mix of happy and unhappy conditions because we encounter a new existence based on our most deeply anchored habits—whether they are linked with desire, attachment, anger, or otherwise— and also based on our karma.

Habits are natural propensities maintained by the mind due to a repetition of the same action. If a person has the tendency to go into churches, his steps naturally guide him toward this edifice. It is a reflex. If the tendency is to go into a café, wherever he is, he will always find a café. We are all made up of our tendencies and the karma that we generate. This is individual and personal. Consciousness is simply colored and influenced by these past habits that push us towards a new life form. These tendencies associate with a direction that is similar to themselves. This is how the process of reincarnation operates. Great Buddhist practitioners do not let themselves be influenced by their habits. This means trying to learn to choose the direction that we wish to take without succumbing to our tendencies. The practice of meditation helps with this, similar to the analysis of our functioning that allows us to change certain predispositions and to create others. Obtaining a human rebirth is thus a question of probability without any certainty whatsoever. It is difficult to believe as a human today that we could become a bird in the next life. And yet, are our convictions truly founded?

When we perceive the color blue, we are convinced of its color. On first glance, we would not believe anyone who holds that blue does not exist. Our perception of things renders them real according to our perspective: perceiving signifies that the object of perception exists. And yet, scientific research, in the context of this example of color, has shown that color itself does not exist. So long as we have not understood the process that leads to our perception of color, our certainty about the existence of blue remains intact.

In the Buddhist context, this stubbornness in believing in the existence of something that, nevertheless, does not exist is named "ignorance." Human rebirth is precious because this condition is endowed with the ability to reflect, analyze, act, and evolve beyond this process of death and rebirth. Yet the majority of humans do not understand or accept this. A sincere Buddhist practice leads to the understanding that, in the same way, our personal dissatisfaction does not truly exist, which allows us to change our vision of suffering and the way that we experience it.

Human existence is also said to be precious because it does not last forever. Thus we must put it to good use. Putting it to the best use possible today means preparing for one's next life. This preparation can be carried out in different ways: by being involved in family life, by deciding to commit fully and essentially to the path of practice, or by combining the two. The majority of people benefit from the pleasant things that life has to offer, on the one hand, while trying to prepare themselves for the next life on the other hand. In any case, the choice is personal.

An observation of human beings allows us to realize that giving in to the impulses of the moment often leads to losing oneself in an endless maze of desires. Ever more numerous and invasive, these desires self-perpetuate. This is how a human being constantly creates its own needs. There is nothing negative about this. However, this mental schema takes root, repeats itself, and eventually becomes anchored to the point of developing into a habit that conditions our very actions, from the most insignificant up through the direction that we give our lives.

Considering human existence allows us to come back to ourselves as a first step. Understanding the potential of being human offers a new look at our condition. Sometimes we wonder about the differences between beings' lives without understanding why some individuals have conditions that are more pleasant than others. In fact, the reason is fairly simple; our current situation is the consequence of acts and tendencies developed in the past. Today, we have this excellent condition of human existence. If we take care of the habits that we develop and make sure to act in a way that is beneficial for ourselves and others, then we are preparing ourselves to pursue our progress on the path, life after life. Even if we cannot grasp all the details of the mechanism of causes and effects—at our level, we cannot clearly see which specific cause brings about which effect—generally understanding the workings of karma already allows us to orient our lives toward the positive and to take care of what occurs in our minds. We also experience less confusion. Indeed, witnessing others' unhappiness can trouble us. We may ask ourselves, "Why me? Why them?" The experience of unhappiness is the result of causes generated in the past. Understanding the workings of karma allows us to act in a more beneficial way. We can continue to progress in this way along the entirety of the path. Do not mistake the implication of cause and effect; the absence of confusion regarding others' suffering does not mean that we should not help them!

## Attachment, Rejection, and Ignorance

Although we are endowed with the potential to evolve toward wisdom, we can observe that we maintain a great attachment to ourselves. This attachment expresses itself in myriad ways: for example, we prioritize things that are pleasant or agreeable to us, and we reject things that bother us. This is what we call duality. In general, each individual thinks that this is simply a matter of human nature, and there is nothing to be done about it. But the teachings explain that therein lies the genesis of unhappiness, of disharmony, and of all that is unpleasant. A mind too carried away by the object of its desire becomes attached to it; the word "object" does not only designate material things, but should be considered in a larger sense. On the contrary, if something repulses this same mind, it immediately wants to distance itself from the object. Between these two extremes, there is a grey area that we do not perceive clearly, a zone of ignorance. Human beings are constantly prey to these three occurrences: attachment, rejection, and ignorance.

The Buddha explains that problems arise from these three occurrences, and this continually disturbs the mind. The natural reaction to this explanation is to try to banish all forms of attachment, rejection, and ignorance, but this is not possible. Indeed, no longer being attached does not depend on an intellectual decision. Freedom from attachment cannot be forced. It only arises as the natural consequence of understanding. This concerns a process which requires time. We cannot erase attachment in the same way that we might flip a switch to turn a light on or off at will. Only a profound integration of the meaning of the teachings allows for natural and authentic change. Several decades ago, no one worried about the pollution caused by cars. We were ignorant of this issue. With the progression of time, and notably the advancement of scientific research, we discovered the chemical composition of pollution and we know much more now. This comprehension triggered a new awareness, and we naturally take more care of the environment now.

The first step consists of becoming aware of the process and noticing in our daily life the way in which we become attached to everything pleasant and reject everything bothersome. Attachment is, in fact, linked with various afflictions: desire, jealousy, pride, etc. Thus, the path begins by taking a neutral look at the way these afflictions emerge and color our perception. We will see that they affect how we perceive others and the situations in which we find ourselves, thus influencing our words and actions. These words and actions equally constitute the causes and thus the consequences we will experience in the future. Through this observation, we understand better that our impulsive actions often push us to react in harmful ways and to experience consequences of the same nature as our actions. We cannot distinguish our own perceptions, and we immediately project judgments on situations or people that lead to attachment, discrimination, and rejection. Understanding this functioning with greater clarity has consequences on two levels. First, we make a greater effort to direct our actions, speech, and thoughts toward benefit and to abstain from causing harm. Second, we understand that this functioning is universal; it is the same for all human beings. By considering the individual, we also achieve a different understanding of what is happening on a collective level.

Detecting the emergence of our emotions, before acting or speaking, allows us to understand what leads us to attachment, rejection, and simply not recognizing the conditions around us. These occurrences constitute the causes that push the mind to get involved with various actions and situations in perpetuity, thus creating infinite complications. All human beings are subject to this basic functioning. This reflection awakens and civilizes our mind, allowing it to gain maturity. Daily life offers us a wealth of useful experiences for perceiving our feelings and noticing our way of communicating with others, as well as all the judgments, expectations, and personal opinions that arise in the mind. If we repeat this exercise with sincerity, we will gain greater clarity and our observation will become increasingly precise. This is already a first step out of confusion and ignorance toward enlightenment.

The term "enlightenment" often resonates with a dimension of fantasy and wonder, while what it signifies is simply being free from all confusion. In the Buddhist context, confusion refers to an absence of clarity and of awareness of the mind's functioning. This renders us dependent on our feelings and opinions and keeps us caught up in a schema for which we alone are responsible. This is the reason why we are constantly dissatisfied and encounter difficulties. Generally speaking, when the train is running late, passengers' first reaction is to get angry. This is a good illustration of confusion. Unaware of the reason for the delay, everyone gives in to the frustration of the moment, which, nevertheless, does not change the situation in the least. This misunderstanding is the source of dissatisfaction. These emotional states make up the fabric of human confusion and we live our lives without knowing why the mind is constantly tense and rarely at peace. Bolstered by this knowledge, we can then seek out the causes that create these disturbances. Once the causes have been identified, it becomes naturally apparent that there is no justification for this tension. It thus dissolves on its own.

It is very simple to achieve this result. The difficulty lies in our involvement with certain circumstances, in our vast knowledge, and in the habits relative to our education and our social, cultural, and simply human context. All of our knowledge and tendencies distract us from what is essential. In addition, we are subject to the circumstances of our environment. All of this easily overwhelms the mind. Becoming aware of these inner happenings allows the mind to become more open and more accepting, which allows us to be less distracted by the difficulties and disturbances of human life. In this way, we become observers of our emotional states, as though we are standing on a bridge overlooking the highway and watching the cars go by at top speed below us. Safe behind the railing of the bridge, we are not in any danger and are thus not worried by the speed of the vehicles below. Our goal is to achieve this same state: to maintain a distance with regard to the emotional and conceptual occurrences that arise within us so that the mind remains relaxed. The objective is to remain constantly in this state rather than simply experiencing it from time-to-time. The happenings of our mind will continue to manifest; they are inherent to the human condition. But we will be less attached to them or will no longer reject them. They will become less difficult and will have a lesser influence on our actions. The mind will be more peaceful, with greater acceptance and less judgment.

Acquiring profound relaxation requires time. It is tempting to want to take shortcuts or skip steps, but this is precisely the attitude that hinders us from obtaining results, as we remain solely on an intellectual level and cannot truly integrate anything beyond concepts.

The mind is accustomed to collecting information and amassing knowledge—causes for confusion. There is nothing wrong with learning or knowledge. That is not the problem. However, we must know that all knowledge accumulated can cause our opinions to become inflexible and lead to confusion if we do not know how to manage this knowledge.

Dissipating this confusion requires us to develop more space in our minds. This is, in part, connected to our physical body—as our perceptions arrive through our sensory faculties—but this is also in direct connection with the mind. We must work with both aspects in order to develop greater relaxation, which leads to more peacefulness. If we do so, the lectures, the teachings received, and the knowledge acquired do not remain simply at an intellectual level. With practice, we experience them differently and we become more disposed to applying them. We become able to refer to them to manage the situations of everyday life that appear both internally and externally. Meditation is the tool that allows us to create and anchor this habit.

The flow of thoughts is continuous, but to begin, let us try to be attentive to the emergence of a new thought in the mind. We will realize that it is connected to a feeling immediately followed by a binary judgment, most often good or bad, beautiful or ugly, pleasant or unpleasant, etc. In Buddhist teachings, there is a lot of discussion of afflictions: desire, attachment, rejection, pride, and so on. However, we do not see how these emotional occurrences take place in the mind because they are instantaneously caught up and carried away by this perpetual flow.

Without becoming aware of this functioning, it is

impossible to remedy it definitively. By remaining with the mind, we can identify a thought and the diverse conditions or circumstances that are connected with it. This work allows us to see how an emotion is activated as well as the manner in which we fully engage with its occurrence. Without this clear understanding, we cannot imagine that we ourselves create our different states of being. Instead, we focus on an external object that we identify as the source of our unhappiness. Though we do not have control over external things, we can, however, see the way in which our minds are completely overtaken by emotions. This influences the way that we act and the future conditions we create. Seeing this process is thus a true understanding of the mind's functioning. All of these occurrences unfold in a very short lapse of time and, as mentioned earlier, thoughts succeed each other without interruption. This complex mechanism applies to every thought, which leads to the daily conceptual and emotional turmoil of our lives. In fact, it all comes down to the occurrences of our thoughts. This understanding allows the mind to become free. Based on this, whether we choose to follow one thought or another is of little importance for we know how to preserve our freedom: all of our perceptions are integrated as occurrences in the mind that thus no longer influence us. We are therefore totally free, all while remaining engaged in life and all that it involves.

Just as this functioning is applicable to us, it is also the lot of all other human beings without exception. We act—we create causes whose consequences we will experience. Remaining focused solely on our own functioning is not sufficient to provide us with answers to all the various situations we encounter. Everyone lives according to different habits and our interactions constitute challenges that fuel the emotional and conceptual occurrences of the mind. Through also considering others, one thing becomes clear: all of us are prisoners of these occurrences in our minds. This understanding leads to a gentler relationship with others, one that is more tolerant and open. This discovery affects our actions and reactions; in other words, we succeed in gaining perspective and developing greater kindness and compassion. In the Buddhist context, the term "compassion" is not only a reference to feeling empathy for those in difficult circumstances. It has a greater meaning: understanding that the diverse living conditions that beings experience are the result of causes that they themselves have created. Compassion is not only an emotional feeling; it requires us to develop integral understanding.

## A Supportive Environment

Surrounding oneself with positive influences encourages this type of introspection. Environment, of course, refers likewise to people as to place. Generally speaking, we rely on our first impression to decide what is good or bad. We lack sufficient reflection to go beyond appearances. It is a little like a commercial designed to have an immediate impact in the mind of the consumer and to generate the desire to acquire the product being sold. In other words, a supportive environment refers to a process; it is not only places and people that are more beneficial than others, but our way of relating to things. Unhelpful places are not always what we might believe or what we would identify as dangerous or suspect. There are places that appear very peaceful, trustworthy, and pleasant, but which are in fact vectors for emotions, disturbances, and distractions, and do not encourage us to reflect on ourselves or to cultivate a compassionate attitude toward others.

Our environment influences us, often without our even noticing. Over the course of the time we spend in one milieu or another, habits form naturally to become trodden paths that we follow automatically. If the milieu is supportive, it influences the mind in a positive way and directs it toward greater clarity and awareness. An unsupportive environment keeps us in confusion, sometimes without us even being aware of it.

Certain great historical practitioners, like Milarepa (1040/1050–1123/1135 CE), preferred to retreat into the mountains and live as hermits to consecrate all of their time to meditation practice. This is a possibility. It is also possible to live a normal life, but with full awareness. This means trying to understand the mind's functioning, the mechanism of beneficial and harmful acts, and the suffering of beings by observing what is happening around us: our way of life, our speech, and our actions. This honest observation allows us to use the opportunity of our human existence in order to improve ourselves and to progress along the path.

With modern means of communication, we are just a click away from one another. This rapidity triggers strong reactions. The mind jumps quickly from one state to another, which does not encourage its stability. If we let this tendency become anchored, we lose all perspective. This results in greater confusion and less openness toward others, and all of our relationships suffer. This does not mean that we must remove ourselves from our environment, but that we must become conscious of the influence that it has over us in order to cultivate effective discernment. Desire, jealousy, anger, pride, and so forth, make up a part of us and are inherent to our human condition. However, certain environments can encourage their development. The idea is to notice. It is normal to desire an object or a person that pleases us, but living solely in this manner is tantamount to drinking salt water—our thirst is never quenched and we always feel as though we need more. It is in this way that our actions and reactions reveal themselves to be completely influenced by the emotional and conceptual occurrences in our mind without our ever realizing it.

## Everything Changes, All the Time

Unhappiness is a recurring subject in the Buddhist teachings. This term is fairly generic and covers experiences from mild discontent to intense physical or mental pain. In fact, it concerns all forms of suffering. What does it mean to be free from unhappiness? Does it simply mean to no longer feel it? Meditation helps to better identify the cause and to more precisely observe our way of living, which constitutes the basis for going beyond suffering step by step. We will come back to this later.

The causes of unhappiness are not external to us; they are born from the mind. Attentive observation allows us to identify them as arising from attachment, jealousy, pride, anger, rejection, etc., and all the expectations that these emotional occurrences generate. The degree of unhappiness is proportional to the degree of attachment to the people or things (house, car, jewelry, clothes, and so on...). In effect, when an expectation is disappointed or foiled, discontent arises most often accompanied by judgment. This is how we create our own unhappiness. It is impossible to force oneself not to suffer; unhappiness is a natural process and inherent to human life. However, it is not a fatality and, as we are in fact at the origin of the process, the good news is that we can neutralize it. Indeed, we are the masters of our way of apprehending situations. This means seeing all of the conditions of a situation with precision, beginning with a reality of which we are all aware: impermanence. Everything changes in every moment and quite unpredictably. Nothing remains the same, whether it is situations, beings, or objects. Thanks to an intimate understanding of this fact, the unhappiness we feel has less strength and can even disappear. The cycle of the seasons is natural. We know that flowers blossom in springtime and fade in the winter. No one gets upset about this or is saddened by it, as we all know that it is the nature of things. Unhappiness continues because of disappointed expectations, because of grasping too tightly to what we want or do not want, and because of our unawareness of the inexorability of impermanence. Changing our point of view will not immediately dissolve the pain connected with losing a loved one, for example, but greater awareness can make loss more comprehensible and contribute to greater acceptance of the current situation.

## The Practice of Bodhisattvas

A bodhisattva is neither a god nor a superhuman. He is an ordinary being who has acquired a more and more exact understanding throughout the course of his path. These human beings can follow a monastic path, be hermits, or carry out an ordinary life as a lay practitioner.

Whatever their lifestyle choice, they have obtained a personal accomplishment in their practice that is notably characterized by the absence of unhappiness. This does not mean denial or naivety regarding the world around them, but full understanding of the causes that create the problems and difficulties of beings. The habit created through training their minds allows them to detect the emergence of an emotion occurring and clearly identify its causes. Strengthened by this clarity, they know that there is no reason to submit to the influence of the emotion. In this way they avoid succumbing to such occurrences. The mechanism that leads to unhappiness is thus undone at its origin.

In the same manner as anybody else, a bodhisattva experiences emotions and thoughts. However, he manages to identify them rapidly and with precision. This dissolves them almost instantaneously because he perceives their absurdity at almost the same speed as the emotions themselves. Sometimes, people think that these realized beings resemble angels, but it is not at all the same thing. They retain their human character and temperament. However, their emotional perceptions no longer disturb the stability and clarity of their minds. Becoming familiar with the path is a process. We cannot change from one day to the next without transition. The path is instead about progressing step by step.

A bodhisattva considers beings in a different way. Indeed, his perception is more subtle and precise than normal and does not change in relation to the fluctuations of his mind. Our perception varies constantly, as though we were drunk. Under the influence of alcohol, our conduct and speech are altered. Once the effects have worn off, we regain our senses. In our case, we are intoxicated by our feelings. Bodhisattvas know that people have negative ideas or act harmfully because their minds are obscured and carried away by different types of emotions. If someone is very attached to his position or his belongings, this state influences his actions and pushes him to act to protect what is important in his eyes. A bodhisattva is aware of this functioning, and this understanding naturally gives rise to compassion within him. Like a doctor who treats illness without judging the worthiness of one patient over another, a bodhisattva adopts the same attitude toward everyone because he sees the causes and conditions at work and knows the reactions and consequences to which they can lead. He understands that everyone is sincere. This universal vision leads to compassion and to an equanimous perception of all beings and thus to greater tolerance. This equanimity is neither forced nor artificial. When it is present, interactions with others become simpler, reactions become less impulsive, and greater harmony appears amongst everyone.

When we manage to see our states of mind, as a bodhisattva does, the problems of daily life lessen because we realize that it is not necessary to worry or be afraid.

To work in this direction, it is not necessary to adopt a particular lifestyle. The only difficulty lies in our amnesia! Indeed, we forget to observe what is happening in our minds as soon as we are confronted with an unhappy situation. The feeling of the moment immediately invades the mind. We do not see that unhappiness is tied to the ego, to jealousy, to attachment, and so forth. The reflex is to embrace what arises in our mind. Our task is thus to change our habits. We must take the time to observe whether what we feel is real or not and to identify the causes—to precisely perceive the connections between the different emotions that generate automatic responses beyond our control. Once we are accustomed to this exercise, we are more aware of the happenings of our mind, and we see more clearly the seeds planted and the effects generated. This analysis reduces the hold our judgments and our feelings have over us, and the emotional and conceptual occurrences of our own minds obscure them to a lesser degree.

This training is not meant to be a source of tension. We must simply apply it consistently and according to the situations that we encounter. Regularity leads to habit. Little by little, as we gain greater clarity, we try to concretely apply this training in relation to our friends and family. We have integrated this practice to some degree when we are able to offer solutions to problems based on the clarity we have gained.

In the late 1970s, a Tibetan teacher by the name of Gendun Rinpoche (1918–1997 CE) settled in Auvergne, France. All those who spent time with him can attest to the same facts: he was always of an even mood and never experienced any suffering. He showed great compassion toward all and did not spare himself when it came to aiding others.

A quick observation allows each of us to reach the same conclusion: life is a series of happy and unhappy moments, of pleasantness and discontent. What makes it possible to remain in a dimension free from these fluctuations? Clarity of mind, in other words, the understanding that there is no reason to suffer. We are constantly running our hands through stinging nettles and yet we are surprised that our fingers are burning! In the same manner that not touching these plants allows us to remain free from their sting, if we do not create the causes that provoke unhappiness, we will not undergo any suffering. The difference between a bodhisattva like Gendun Rinpoche and ourselves lies in the fact that he knows the causes to apply to be happy and those to avoid in order not to suffer.

The goal of taking the bodhisattva's path is to become, ourselves, like Gendun Rinpoche. For example, to obtain profound serenity and a clarity of mind that allows us to be truly useful to others. Compassion is the natural result of profound understanding. Indeed, developing compassion does not mean adding an ingredient; rather, compassion results simply from personal integration of the meaning of our human condition. When we understand that all beings are subject to the same functioning and create the causes for their own unhappiness, we acquire a discernment that is not subject to egocentric, emotional impulses and which thus leaves space for a new mode of being. Forcing oneself into compassion does not work. Authentic and efficacious compassion appears naturally.

Chapter 2

# Reference Points

The work of examining the state of affairs previously described gives rise to a profound understanding of the functioning of human beings and of our inherent life conditions. The value of human existence is seen from more than a purely material standpoint. In present-day society, it is important to make choices and take responsibilities that contribute to a certain form of security (financial, familial, etc.). We also appreciate having a life that is pleasant, where we can have fun and enjoy ourselves. Buddhism goes beyond this and proposes adding long-term security by taking into account not only this life, but those to come.

Ensuring that we will have good conditions up to our deaths is one thing, but Buddhism proposes assurance for future lives as well. This is why we work toward having good relative conditions in the present life, and we likewise lay the groundwork—on the level of the mind—to obtain security in the long-term, so as not to have to encounter future difficulties.

Through becoming aware of the changing and un-predictable nature of all phenomena, of the value of human existence, and of the mechanism of cause-and-effect, we can work toward freeing ourselves from the confusion that naturally fogs our perception of reality. If we wish to follow this path and orient our life in this direction, some points of reference are useful to facilitate our progress and prevent us from getting off track and wasting time.

In Buddhism, the principal reference point is called "taking refuge" and includes three aspects. The expression "to take refuge" somewhat misrepresents its literal meaning. In Tibetan, it concerns more specifically going toward protection—that of the Buddha, the methods, and all those who have realized them and put them into practice. In life, nothing and no one can offer material, external protection that is permanent and stable. How are the Buddha, his teaching, and the community of ac-complished practitioners different? First, Buddha is not a god that we worship who can deliver us from our con-dition if we please him or create obstacles for us if we displease him. He is the example of a man who made his way, step by step, until he discovered how to put a definitive end to unhappiness, in other words, until he attained enlightenment. Second, his teaching is not a dogma; it is made up of various methods to apply and test in relation to our own affinity for one or another method, in order to ourselves become Buddhas. The teaching is a concept to understand and apply. And last, accomplished practitioners who have walked this path themselves and applied its methods are the guides and sources of inspiration, in the image of the bodhisattvas. This protection is different than those with which we are already familiar because it does not operate from the outside. We must establish it within ourselves.

The Buddha, his methods, and those who have accomplished them—who embody and transmit them—constitute the points of reference and a guiding principle to integrate into our daily lives, without any limits of age, physical condition, intellectual capacity, social class, or gender...the refuge is universal and is available for everyone. The message is simple, but understanding it can take time. That depends on each of us.

What is enlightenment? A stable state free from all unhappiness. In this state, the mind is clear that there is no longer any reason to be overtaken by confusion or to create the conditions for suffering. This state does not appear over the course of a week-long seminar. It is a long journey, and it is important to be aware that right up to the end of the path, we will continue to encounter the difficulties inherent to our imperfect existence.

Taking refuge is a method that can lead to definitive freedom from suffering through realizing enlightenment. Other paths allow one to achieve certain levels of accomplishment, but not the state of Buddhahood. It is interesting to note that the goal of meditation practice in Mahayana Buddhism (called The Great Vehicle), which we follow here, is to lead the practitioner himself to become a Buddha. In the ancient schools of Indian Buddhism, it was never a question of attaining enlightenment. Based on the methods proposed, practitioners of these schools were able to achieve very high levels of accomplishment, such as liberation, but never complete and perfect enlightenment.

## The Buddha

Why should we wish to become a Buddha? What does definitive freedom from suffering mean? These two points are crucial, and we often do not take the necessary time to reflect on them. When we experience severe unhappiness, we wish—from the deepest part of our being—to be completely free from suffering. But the instant our problem is solved, the necessity of attaining enlightenment is no longer as pressing and our daily functioning takes over once again. It is therefore important to reflect, to observe what happens within us and around us, and to compare this with the Buddha's words. In this way it is possible to deeply anchor a direction within ourselves.

Before attaining enlightenment, the Buddha carried out extensive research. He observed how beings live and the things to which they are subject, what their conditions truly are. He saw that birth, old age, sickness, and death are states inherent to human beings. This observation seems obvious, and yet we often do not truly consider its ramifications. This fact is the reason we are not truly free and are prisoners of the circumstances that we create: karma, on the one hand, and the conditions around us on the other. Having personally become aware of this, Shakyamuni Buddha sought a solution. He tried a variety of approaches until discovering one that provides definitive freedom from this functioning. In this way, the Buddha attained enlightenment at the conclusion of his meditative path. Therefore, we can see that it is useful to look at daily life, observe different lifestyles—our own and those of others, and not only based on the last few years, but on a larger scale—and to consider things as a whole.

This observation combined with the methods proposed, notably that of the refuge, allows one to begin to put an end to unhappiness and to the difficulties we encounter. No one directly seeks suffering, but, quite unintentionally, we act without taking into account the consequences of our actions. Karma functions like a plant: when we sow a seed, it will grow when all of the conditions for its proper development come together. In its own time, it blossoms and produces seeds of its own that nestle into the earth and sprout again, etc. Human beings such as ourselves and life as we experience it are the results of the meeting of our karma and the surrounding circumstances.

The Buddha did not invent anything. He simply described the natural process of life and explained its functioning without error or exaggeration, including its beneficial and harmful aspects. We therefore take refuge in the Buddha as the source of this discovery. Shakyamuni Buddha did not spread his discovery or his methods himself; he simply responded to the questions asked of him and the requests made so that his explanations could be beneficial for others. All of his responses lead in the same direction: definitive freedom from unhappiness. Sentient beings aspire to conditions of happiness. We all try, unskillfully, to acquire them, and this works temporarily, but never in the long-term. We take refuge in the Buddha because he succeeded in permanently realizing this state beyond all unhappiness. He thus represents the possibility of this achievement.

In Tibetan, the term "Buddha[6]" is composed of two syllables with individual meanings. The first signifies that the Buddha has surpassed the ordinary emotional and conceptual functioning of a human being. He is no longer subject to confusion. The second syllable indicates that he has developed the qualities of his mind to their fullest extent. Due to his journey—in other words, the process of recognizing and wearing out the functioning of ordinary mind—he has freed himself from ignorance and gained clarity. These two aspects function like the two sides of a scale: if there is less confusion, there is greater clarity. All sentient beings are endowed with this same clear and knowing potential, also called Buddha nature. In other words, every individual is capable of becoming a Buddha because this potential is inherent to the nature of sentient beings. If we succeed in pacifying the occurrences that disturb the mind, such as different emotions, opinions, fixed ideas, and habits, then we gain discernment and clarity of mind, as well as developing a certain wisdom. Thus, we take refuge in the Buddha because he embodies qualities free from all confusion.

We often have the feeling of understanding something the first time we hear it. This is no different for the concepts we are developing here. However, there remains an issue with this: what we have heard does not bring about significant evolution in our daily life. Therein lies the heart of the problem. We understand many things, but our hearing is conditioned; it is dependent on other understanding acquired previously, on our educa-

---

6    Phonetic: *sangye*, Wylie: *sangs rgyas*

tion, on social, familial, and professional context, etc. A Buddha's knowledge is not governed by these confused mechanisms. His mind is totally independent. Through perseverance and effort, a person can acquire profound knowledge of a subject, in the manner of a research scientist. However, one's perfect mastery of a subject does not mean that he is omniscient and immune to error. In the case of a Buddha, it is not a process of acquiring knowledge, but a state of mind: a quality of perception that remains unobscured by any veils, be they emotional, karmic, cognitive, or habit-based. He thus knows everything, as a whole and in detail. He is no longer influenced by "himself" as we are. The process of becoming a Buddha consists in coming back to the source—our own nature free from all extraneous veils. We take refuge in this state of the fullness of qualities in order to be able to realize it in our own right. When we choose to follow a path, it is useful to know where it leads. It is therefore useful to be aware of the qualities of what we seek to become.

In this world, many people have great clarity of mind. What is the difference, then, between these people and a Buddha? A Buddha does not experience unhappiness. An ordinary human being, such as a genius, may have great qualities, but he experiences suffering: he falls prey to his emotions and to confusion at other levels, and he commits errors. A Buddha does not experience suffering because his mind is so clear that the conditions for suffering do not arise in his consciousness.

In connection with this clarity of mind, it is interesting to note that the Buddha's great discernment allowed him to describe life forms that exist within magma as well as in the world's coldest zones and the depths of the ocean. These descriptions have been confirmed recently by modern scientific research. The Buddha agreed to explain the methods we need to apply to change our conditions. Nothing and no one judges our acts and decides to punish or reward us. Our experience is simply a process set off by fundamental ignorance, which results in us following our individual perceptions and sensations. In this way, we create an abundance of karmic causes of different natures that result in our different life conditions. A Buddha perceives reality because his knowledge does not pass through the filter of obscuration related to himself or to egocentric functioning. Compassion—openness toward others—automatically accompanies clarity of mind. A Buddha no longer has the egocentric reflex to consider things in regards to himself; he is entirely focused on others.

Once again, taking the time to examine what a Buddha is and what this term signifies in the context of the refuge contributes to a solid foundation. Approaching the question from different angles—the aspect of the man—Shakyamuni Buddha, that of a state of mind and its qualities, and that of the result of a process—allows for an overall vision.

## The Methods

The second aspect of the refuge is that of the methods or teachings, called Dharma in Sanskrit. This refers to the path shown by the Buddha. His view can be summarized in four points: composite phenomena are impermanent; all that is characterized by grasping is unhappiness; all phenomena are free and empty of a self; unhappiness is entirely absent in the state beyond suffering. A bodhisattva applies these points and accomplishes benefit for himself and others by not causing harm and by mastering his own mind.

The teachings are not rules we must follow to the letter, but advice to put into practice in life. They constitute reference points that we can come back to in order to see if what we are doing is in accord with the direction of enlightenment or not. Everything depends on the quality of attention to and awareness of what we are doing. Indeed, most of the time, we follow the movement of the majority. We act based on the example of those around us and of our environment. Coming back to the Buddha's teaching allows us to acquire discernment regarding our way of being and acting. We can thus verify whether we are going in the direction of enlightenment or if, on the contrary, we are reinforcing habits that cultivate our own unhappiness. Becoming familiar with the concepts of the Dharma leads to becoming aware of the acts that we carry out. This, then, allows us to prioritize things that are beneficial.

Life is always a mix of beneficial and harmful acts. Gaining discernment allows us to understand situations as they truly are, with fewer emotional and cognitive filters. We can then try to find positive responses to the situations we encounter. Life is not a bad thing that we must surpass or turn away from; on the contrary, the goal is to live fully, and the condition for this to be possible is to strive for that which is beneficial. This is, in fact, what creates positive conditions. Sticking to this guideline is at times a challenge, particularly in an information age where the rapidity and sheer quantity of data transmitted can often create more confusion than clarity. It is tempting to let oneself be influenced and to give in to the ambient discontent, or to fear or anxiety. However, nothing is ever black or white. A whole palette of gray makes up our universe.

When the Buddha's teaching emphasizes that all sentient beings act negatively, this does not mean that we are bad. In complete innocence, we act to satisfy our basic needs, but also our desires. Often we do so without asking ourselves too many questions and later we are surprised to find ourselves facing difficulties.

The Buddhist teaching offers an approach to situations that allows the mind to be more relaxed and less controlled by fear, which facilitates relationships with others. The Dharma considers, in particular, ignorance and the fact that the mind gets carried away by the continuous flow of conceptual and emotional occurrences. It becomes colored by this influence and, in the end, acts based on its impetus. One of the methods the Buddha taught consists of carrying out an observation of what is happening within us. The continuum of our thoughts and acts becomes visible little by little. In this way, through gaining clarity, confusion dissolves. On the basis of this understanding, everything becomes more pleasant and agreeable.

The application of the Dharma always begins with great expectations and a form of excitement. This calms down with time, and it is important to be aware of this fact so as not to be disappointed. These methods demand time, just as a habit requires more than a day to take root. To look at what is happening in the mind, we must succeed in calming the mind and clarifying the occurrences that traverse it. This is why the Buddha taught meditation methods. We will discuss these techniques in greater detail in a later chapter. Regular application of meditation changes the way we perceive things. Furthermore, this moment of solitary introspection offers perspective on situations where others are involved. We can reconsider our interactions and better understand the origin of our disturbances. If we do not remain with a superficial view, but contemplate our connections with others more deeply and with honesty, we will see that the source of our disturbances does not come from others, but from ourselves: satisfied or disappointed expectations, desires, and anger. Beginning by applying the methods of the Dharma to ourselves allows us to understand what ignorance is and how the illusion that conditions our karma arises. Another aspect also appears clearly: others are subject to the same inner workings as we are.

Through practice, a natural understanding arises, even in regard to unpleasant people! Our mind becomes wiser and more tolerant. The spiritual path becomes clear over the course of its application. We must experience the teachings in our daily life. If not, there will always be a gap between our knowledge of the methods, on the one hand, and life, on the other hand. The goal is to live the Buddha's teaching. Life does not become perfect, but it naturally takes the direction of benefit and moves away from the causes of suffering.

Buddhist practice prioritizes personal observation connected to the Buddha's teachings in order to avoid simply superimposing a judgment or individual opinion on the object of our reflection.

Doubts and confusion can appear naturally; they will dissolve over time as our vision becomes clearer and gains precision. Clarity facilitates progress on the path: once the meaning is understood, it is useless to expend effort in order to maintain a direction. Instead, this becomes a spontaneous orientation that does not meet with inner resistance.

The key lies in the quality of stability that we develop. Indeed, if the mind succeeds in remaining calm and serene, it is no longer the toy of the situations that it encounters. It does not trigger the mechanism that generates unhappiness. The method of the Dharma offers responses other than those dictated by our tendencies. The Buddha gave several types of teachings as humans have diverse capacities, temperaments, and characters. For this reason, different schools of Buddhism exist, each one emphasizing a specific method. We choose one or another based on our affinity. However, once we have taken a direction, the goal is to understand its aim and to apply it in order to the obtain the intended result.

Taking refuge in the Dharma is not a matter of listening to pretty words. Rather, it means embodying the meaning of the teaching in our lives. By taking the Dharma as a reference and applying its methods, we can develop the qualities of a Buddha and achieve a definitive solution to unhappiness.

## Traveling Companions

Learning these methods cannot be done solely by reading a book. The example of those who have walked the path before us offers a reference point—encouragement and a necessary source of inspiration on this road. Taking refuge in the Sangha, or the community of accomplished practitioners, means looking to qualified people to help us understand the meaning of the Buddhist teaching and to progress along the path. In other words, it means realizing the same capacities as these practitioners by following their example, as did the bodhisattvas.

The teacher plays an essential role in this process, as he transmits and explains the meaning of the teaching and its methods of application. In *The Jewel Ornament of Liberation*, the master Gampopa insists on the qualities of such a teacher. He must have comprehensive knowledge of the Buddha's words, he must be capable of responding to all questions regarding the Dharma, and he must, himself, apply and live what he teaches. Such a teacher is said to be ordinary; he guides our steps on the path of the bodhisattvas, but he is likewise on the path and progresses in the same manner.

Numerous people acquire strong knowledge of the Dharma. As for any subject, developing an intellectual and theoretical understanding is within everyone's reach. However, a scholar is not necessarily a good teacher. Indeed, the application of the teaching is just as important. If the teacher does not, himself, apply what he explains, his transmission remains incomplete and the student cannot attain all the qualities of the teaching. This problem is likewise possible as a student; listening to the Buddha's words without applying them will not allow one to obtain the intended result. We will simply acquire an intellectual understanding that will not transform our basic functioning. For the teacher, as for the student, the phase of concrete application is the element that guarantees the authenticity of the result.

There is also another type of teacher known as an "extraordinary" teacher. Such teachers are heroes, not because they have superpowers but because they embody the Buddha's teaching and the sole goal of their lives is to accomplish the benefit of beings. These teachers are bodhisattvas who have such a complete mastery and accomplishment of the Dharma that they are free from all confusion. All of their actions are free from personal intention and dedicated to helping others. These model teachers offer us a source of inspiration for the entirety of the path.

Their biographies are useful tools. They reveal that these bodhisattvas lived only the teaching and lived it fully. Some of these bodhisattvas dwelled in miserable conditions without this being a source of suffering or a problem. Others, by contrast, enjoyed conditions of abundance without any attachment to their lifestyles. These diverse examples allow us to understand the essence of practice on the Buddhist path. Bodhisattvas can be ordinary humans of flesh and blood; only their state of mind differentiates them from others. Their minds are, indeed, more relaxed and imbued with greater wisdom. The absence of fear, worry, and unhappiness gives them great capacities to aid others. A mind that is not subject to emotional and conceptual fluctuations is balanced and available for others.

Taking refuge in these beings means following the same direction and developing in their image. Sometimes, we do not know how to identify what is beneficial or useful in the long-term and we take the path that seems the quickest or offers the most enticing results in the short-term. This does not mean that we are taking a wrong direction, but simply that we are orienting ourselves toward something other than unlimited benefit that is not subject to impermanence.

A bodhisattva is a person whose mind is filled with kindness and compassion and whose acts are destined solely to benefit others. He wishes to improve himself and develop his qualities based solely on the motivation of being able to help those in need. The goal of progressing is not for any personal satisfaction but toward the perfection of his qualities for others' benefit. A bodhisattva clearly perceives beings' hardships and the causes of problems as well as their consequences. He thus wishes to make the means to surpass them—both temporarily and definitively—available. With this objective clearly in mind, he does not stray from the path, whatever obstacles or circumstances he meets along the way.

By following the example of these excellent companions, we are sure to take a beneficial direction for others, and also for ourselves. Pure motivation, attitude, and application comprise a stable foundation for developing oneself. Daily complications no longer bother us. We thus manage to choose the method appropriate for us and to put it into practice until it becomes second nature and fully takes root within us.

Whatever situations and difficulties bodhisattvas face, they always act beneficially. This activity is not temporary or provisional. A person who wishes to undertake a spiritual path should be clear concerning the result that he wishes to obtain and the means to apply in order to achieve his goal. This reflection gives us the opportunity to reconsider our priorities in life and the time that we devote to different activities. Some tasks are quite demanding in terms of time, but are they really useful? Clarifying our intention and our degree of commitment is necessary; otherwise we may struggle with contradictions between our aspirations and what we put in place to accomplish them. The bodhisattvas help us, but they cannot walk the path in our place. It is thus important to know what we want in the long-term. This analysis does not take place solely before committing to the path. It is a view of ourselves that we must consider again and again in order to ensure that our actions are truly in accord with our aspirations.

These companions, who are much further along the path than ourselves, are also the guarantee of an environment with a beneficial influence. If we wish to develop qualities identical to theirs, being surrounded by this type of person is ideal. The place and the people that make up our environment influence us in one direction or another. If kindness and compassion are the qualities that we wish to develop, connecting to the bodhisattvas or to a spiritual master who teaches and cultivates these values will help reveal our own capacities and orient our attitude in this direction. By maintaining a virtuous state of mind, we create a current of positivity that tends naturally toward the beneficial. The reverse is also possible. Bad habits inevitably lead to other bad habits. It is not a question of being beyond reproach from one day to the next, but of taking care of our states of mind and being aware of our actions. Recognizing a harmful intention or action allows us to amend it and to aspire to react differently in the future, which generates an upward, positive spiral. We can carry out this exercise for ourselves but also for others. Indeed, the power of the wishes we make that others act beneficially reinforces the positive current in our own minds and likewise has an effect on our environment.

## The Link between Life and the Cushion

Taking refuge in the Buddha, the methods—in other words the Dharma—and the Sangha, the community of bodhisattvas, is not a practice reserved for beginners or for a particular moment in the day. It is not a matter of a sentence to repeat, but a reference to keep in mind, whatever we are doing. This is how the refuge develops from an external point of reference to become integrated into our lives and our minds. The quality of being present to what we are doing changes imperceptibly. A direction naturally takes root within us through the simple fact of being vigilant and recalling the refuge. Progress occurs like this—without delineated steps or discernible levels, but rather in the little nothings of daily life, in the link between life and the cushion.

Beginners often imagine that spiritual practice is reserved for the cushion, in a calm and soothing place ideal for meditation and concentration. This vision of spiritual practice is incomplete. In fact, practice is a matter of bringing the concepts acquired in the teaching hall into our daily lives. Taking refuge does not mean bowing before a statue or setting out offerings, but rather creating the mental habit of the refuge as a point of reference. This natural presence allows us to act like a bodhisattva. Then, there is no longer any difference between sitting on a cushion or being in daily life. In the beginning, a form of separation is normal, but it dissipates over time as we develop the habit. Through connecting all that we do with the notions of the refuge and the Buddhist teaching, we spontaneously become more inclined toward kindness and compassion. This point is important because it gives a stable direction to our lives.

Each of us has the potential to become a Buddha. Fully realizing this potential is not easy, but by taking refuge in the Buddha, we can begin to follow the right direction and to progress until we achieve this state over time. Taking refuge in the Dharma allows us to avoid suffering through understanding the causes that create it, and, based on a profound commitment, to evolve up through enlightenment. To follow this path, we require the example of those who have already committed to it, in the past and in the present day. Even if we cannot act exactly as they do, we can, nonetheless, take inspiration from their example in order to develop ourselves.

Chapter 3

# Kindness and Compassion

Kindness and compassion are the central elements of the practice of bodhisattvas.

A solid comprehension of the mechanisms that engender unhappiness as well as good knowledge of our schemas of functioning are necessary prerequisites for considering the notions of kindness and compassion. Bodhisattvas are a source of inspiration for generating these qualities. It is not a matter of copying them, but of taking their way of thinking, communicating, and acting as a reference. These role models are not exclusive to Buddhism and also exist on other spiritual paths; for example, in the form of saints in Catholicism.

## Taking Care of Ourselves

Various motivations can push us to seek a spiritual path. In general, the wish to resolve problems or free ourselves from difficulties—in  other words, to go beyond unhappiness—pushes us to seek out methods.

When we have attained the objectives that we have fixed for ourselves, we experience some satisfaction or even great happiness, depending on the strength of the feeling. However, it is also clear that this happiness does not last. We find new directions and gravitate toward other goals to accomplish. The contentment of having achieved a certain result gives way to a subsequent dissatisfaction. This is nothing surprising; it is simply human nature.

When we have solely positive conditions and everything is going our way, things are fine. However, as soon as a grain of sand slips into the gears, everything seizes up—our mind, for starters. This results in arguments, negative thoughts, harmful actions, and diverse individual disturbances that likewise have repercussions at a collective level: that of a family, a group of friends, a country, etc., and which can even degenerate into war. It is important—without having to arrive at this catastrophic scenario—to become aware that these two aspects are always intimately linked: the individual and the collective.

Despite a profound wish to meet only with happiness, we maintain ourselves in perpetual combat that has repercussions on our environment. The Buddha's teaching explains that a harmful act may indeed allow us to achieve a desired result; however, this act leaves an imprint that will resurface later on. The Buddha called this process karma.

Karma can be divided into a series of events: firstly, a thought arises and crystallizes into an intention. From this mental occurrence, an act unfolds—words or action. This act operates as a cause which will have a consequence of identical nature. If the nature of our thoughts, our intentions, and our actions is beneficial, then we do not have to worry. However, if we are constantly sowing harmful seeds, we must be aware that we will experience unpleasant consequences.

Karma is made up of the force of the mind's intention, the act itself, and its result. This process operates on the long-term as well as in every moment, which makes it difficult to observe. It is nonetheless unavoidable for each of us. We sow seeds, instant after instant, either beneficial, harmful, or neutral. If we do not develop awareness, we perpetuate this mechanism and the causes of our unhappiness and continue pushing lasting happiness further out of our reach. This is why the Buddha invites us to take care of ourselves.

We can take care of ourselves on a physical level, by taking care to eat and sleep well, exercising regularly, etc. In this way, we improve our health and avoid illness. Paying attention to one's environment also means taking care of oneself. In Buddhism, there is an additional dimension: taking care of our minds. This means becoming aware of what arises so that we do not simply follow the emotional and conceptual occurrences taking place. If we do not take care, certain thoughts or feelings can degenerate and wind up controlling our actions. Following the Dharma does not mean forcing ourselves or imposing restrictions, but, instead, simply being attentive to our thoughts to prevent them from negatively influencing our words and actions.

The majority of our problems stem from desire and attachment, both sources of great complication in life. One point is worth clarifying to avoid misinterpretation: the Buddha's teaching does not ask us to eliminate desire or attachment. It explains that their presence triggers a process. Often, in the West as in Asia, practitioners have the understanding that we must erase them. Desire and attachment are not bad or negative in and of themselves, but as with any affliction, they color the mind and influence our actions, often in a self-centered way. This emotional disturbance interferes with our vigilance and we no longer pay attention to what we are doing. This is generally how we wind up acting in a harmful way.

Desire and attachment are like rotten food. The problem is not with the food itself, but rather with the fact that it is spoiled and thus acts like a poison if we ingest it.

Remaining in the grasp of this emotional occurrence perturbs us continually and hinders us from developing another vision of things. So what do we do when we identify this functioning? The example of great bodhisattvas comes into play. Bodhisattvas are not content to simply recognize the presence of desire and attachment; they also understand that it is empty of essence.

One of the first teachings given by the Buddha is called *Placing the Focus Closest to Four [Objects]*, frequently translated as *The Four Objects of Mindfulness*[7].

---

7   For further explanations on this teaching, see: Rinpoche, Kunzig Shamar. Kunzig Shamar Rinpoche: *The Four Foundations of Mindfulness*. DVD. Saint Léon-sur-Vézère, France: Dhagpo Kagyu Ling, 2015.

The examination of the body, sensations, mind, and phenomena leads to understanding the senselessness of attachment. In this way, we become free from its hold, similar to the image of a child's attachment to his toys. There comes a day when he no longer shows any interest in them, regardless of how strong his initial feelings for them may have been.

We emphasize attachment here because we experience it in a way that is real and present and because it constitutes the principal cause of our unhappiness. Reflecting on and examining the mechanism of attachment brings greater flexibility of mind. The same goes for pride, anger, etc. The Buddha's teaching does not push us to eradicate pride. On the contrary, it is a motor for attaining objectives in life. The teaching invites us, rather, to recognize the dangers that it can present. Pride can lead to the mind being rigid, and to rejecting certain things while only adopting those that suit us and ignoring others, etc. We must try to observe our minds, not only when all is well—when we are relaxed and calm—for this is not very efficient, but also when there is agitation. We see the most interesting things when the mind is a bit disturbed or dissatisfied. These slight experiences of unpleasantness do not seem very important on first look, but through analyzing them, we refine our vision. Regular training does not resolve all of our problems immediately, but it can bring about change over time.

Our general reflex is to look at outward, external conditions. In contrast with this habit, we need to look inward, at the mind itself. For example, we will notice that, when our pride is confronted with certain circumstances, it becomes activated and reacts. Recognizing this process defuses it and neutralizes its influence on the mind. We can see the same scenario with all other emotions. We are never trained to have emotions; no one taught them to us. It is simply a matter of the habitual functioning of our minds. Through distinguishing emotional triggers, we can cause this ordinary process to retreat, and another perception takes its place. The mind shifts its gaze from being focused solely on itself and opens toward others. A different understanding establishes itself and communication with others also improves.

In certain publications, we come across the expression "transforming emotion into wisdom." It is important to understand that this does not function like an electrical switch. We cannot simply decide to hit the button "wisdom" or "emotion" at will. Neither does this phrase mean to paint over an emotion with artificial or fabricated wisdom. The terminology can sometimes cause errors in understanding. One must simply perceive that, if we are not attentive, emotional and conceptual occurrences can lead to harmful actions. When we understand and recognize the functioning, then there is no longer confusion, but wisdom.

Taking care of ourselves means changing our reflexes to ask the right questions: what is really happening? How would a bodhisattva act in this same situation? How can I adapt to this situation based on my understanding? Our automatisms do not transform immediately, but our vision changes little by little. Meaning emerges, which creates freedom of mind, a space that offers perspective and allows us to take note of what is happening.

While individuals' tendencies may vary in intensity, our functioning is nevertheless identical. Others can thus become a reference point or a mirror for ourselves. Realizing this makes us, in turn, more understanding and also reveals certain of our own emotional games to us. In this way, instead of succumbing to the immediate vivid emotion, we can gain distance and not react in the heat of the moment. Over the course of this training, our attitudes and actions change.

So many things happen in so little time in the mind! Observation does not prove as easy as one might imagine. Thus, we must place our attention on daily life and contemplate our way of thinking, acting, communicating, and perceiving others, while taking the Buddha's teaching as a reference point. In the beginning, the mental categorizations that we are constantly creating, and which solidify into fixed ideas, hinder authentic perception of situations and beings. The sole objective of observation is to give rise to an awareness of our impulsive and immediate schemas and judgments. They have repercussions on our speech and actions and bring about consequences. An understanding of karmic functioning supports this process. This approach naturally orients us toward a beneficial state of mind and, as a result, harmful actions likewise diminish.

As we have already emphasized several times, this process takes time and its success depends on the sincerity of the observation we apply to ourselves (without culpability or discouragement). We will not become totally perfect, but great changes can occur.

According to the Buddha's teachings, the suffering that sentient beings experience is simply the result of harmful seeds planted. It is important to keep in mind that this is neither a judgment nor a punishment. No one decides to condemn others to perpetual unhappiness because of harmful actions. It is simply the mechanical functioning of karma. Though we do not have much latitude concerning the result in this process, we can, however, act upon the cause.

The world is peopled by multitudes of beings with extremely varied life conditions. Certain beings endure atrocious suffering while others enjoy pleasant circumstances. This is neither random chance nor injustice. Beings created the causes for these conditions in the past, and these causes now simply give their results. Such things may happen to any of us if we do not take care of our minds.

This observation helps to anchor the decision to cause as little harm as possible and also to take care of others. A genuine view of the causes of beings' suffering—ignorance of karmic functioning and lack of attention—modifies our perception of others. The mind opens to a dimension of kindness and compassion.

## Enlightened Mind

The kindness and compassion in question grow from profound personal understanding, and not emotional, exclusive feeling. They concern the wish that all beings experience happiness and its causes and become free from unhappiness and its causes. A bodhisattva conforms fully and solely to this wish, in thought, speech, and action toward all beings, without any preferences.

Applying equanimous kindness and compassion to everyone seems difficult when the aspect of emotion comes into play. Here, kindness and compassion are not a matter of feeling empathy toward a particular person. A bodhisattva develops kindness and compassion toward all, without exception or judgment.

Kindness and compassion, also called enlightened mind, are based on subtle knowledge and not on feelings. Emotional compassion can very quickly transform into aggression. Indeed, if we only cultivate sentimental feelings, they can fluctuate according to the circumstances and potentially transform into their opposite, just like any occurrence in the mind. Enlightened mind, as developed by bodhisattvas, is a precise perception of the life conditions of beings. This understanding does not arise instantaneously, but must be constructed over the course of the path.

Observing fishermen on the beach or the bank of a river is a good teaching. While the fish is still wriggling—alive—the fisherman sticks a knife in its gut and cuts off its head. Seeing this spectacle for the first time is shocking and provokes a natural compassion toward the animal (relative to the disposition of the individual). However, if this spectacle makes up part of our daily life, it becomes banal, normal. Over time, we do not feel anything upon seeing this act. The opposite may even occur: the sight might make us salivate over the thought of delicious, fresh fish, to the point that we might become fishermen ourselves. The daily repetition of this experience anesthetizes our feeling. This example is not meant to criticize fishermen, but to illustrate the functioning of ignorance and the development of habits. Compassion must be founded on understanding. It then becomes a matter of cultivating it and anchoring it in our daily experience. If we do not develop and cultivate compassion based on understanding, we will not be able to progress. Attentive observation of our environment and of its impact on the mind is an important part of the path. It is, after all, easy to let ourselves be taken in by the emotional discourse to which we are accustomed. This can cause us to lose the beneficial potential of kindness and compassion. It is not a question of distancing oneself strictly from a milieu or an environment, but rather of maintaining vigilance and trying to draw conclusions from our observations in order to progress along the path.

Kindness and compassion are qualities inherent to human nature. In Europe, for example, we can see that these basic concepts exist based on concern for social, environmental, and health issues. Trying to reduce physical and ethical suffering is part of enlightened mind. However, another quality must be applied: discernment. Sometimes, the absence of knowledge or of a global view of a situation can lead to causing errors. This is how a beneficial intention can give rise to an act that is not beneficial (the act may even be the opposite—harmful) through a lack of discernment. This is nothing more than the expression of human nature. The initial intention is good, but it does not bring about the desired result. We acquire greater discernment by referring to the Buddha's teaching and to the understanding of karma in particular.

Positive intention alone is not sufficient to act beneficially. First, we must attain perspective in order to be sure of the impact of the act. On this basis, we can decide whether or not to take the opportunity to act. The teachings constitute a reference to the extent that they explain how to apply certain things and avoid others in order to refrain from harming ourselves or negatively affecting others. It is a matter of gaining clarity of mind to have greater discernment and, therefore, appropriate actions. Meditation helps with this. We will develop this point in the following chapter.

Kindness and compassion can be considered on a relative level, as a rule of moral conduct that we adopt in daily life, but they can also be considered in terms of the state of mind that leads to enlightenment. This, then, concerns a different degree of commitment, which allows for the activation of great potential. On the path toward enlightenment, the focal point shifts from ourselves to others. As we are no longer the center of our preoccupations, situations, beings, and difficulties no longer bother us as much. This does not mean that we can be negligent. We must, like everyone, face the problems that we encounter, but they will affect us much less. Life is therefore simpler, and our actions become more efficient and beneficial.

Based on living a simple life oriented solely toward others, bodhisattvas develop greater-than-average capacities. This level of accomplishment is neither miracle nor magic, but the progressive development of enlightened mind. The application of kindness and compassion in conjunction with discernment allows us to become more independent from the ordinary concepts of daily life and, in addition, to augment the extent and efficiency of our actions. An intentionally beneficial action accomplished with altruistic motivation combine to create positive conditions for the future.

The choice to apply a relative aspect of kindness and compassion in order to have a personal ethic or to commit more deeply so that this kindness and compassion become a path to enlightenment depends on the individual. Certain people wish to concentrate on the present life, managing this existence in a beneficial way until it reaches its end. This is a possibility. In this case, a path of relative kindness and compassion is sufficient. Other people worry about what happens following death without really knowing, while still others already have in mind their next destination. For these individuals, the Buddha's teaching invites us to take care of our current life to prepare for those to come. Our concern for what happens after death functions in a similar way to our preoccupation for the environment. Concerning the environment, certain people do not see the necessity of protecting it and act without paying attention, others understand that certain precautions are necessary, and still others educate themselves to fully understand the future consequences and thus worry about ecological conditions. The level of attention is proportional to the level of knowledge of the subject.

The same goes for our own lives. If we understand the conditions of our current life (which includes our thoughts, speech, and actions) and we see the results they will have in the future, we wake up to their implications. We realize that we cannot neglect the process of karma because our next life depends on it. Understanding the meaning of unhappiness and its causes is necessary for the development of enlightened mind.

As emphasized previously, motivation and intention are important, but they must be accompanied by discernment when acting. A bodhisattva, through training and practice, acquires capacities that make him truly useful and beneficial. For the moment, we are prisoners of our tendencies, which prevents us from having an elevated level of kindness and compassion. If we succeed in fully realizing the quality of enlightened mind, then, in the image of the bodhisattvas, we can be useful and efficient for all beings. If not, the reach of our actions remains limited and uncertain.

It is thus a matter of taking the time to reflect in order to clearly understand what the notion of enlightened mind and its application comprise. Ideas abound in the mind, but patience is a must in order to verify what is truly beneficial before committing ourselves to an action whose outcome we do not control. Otherwise, we will retain a functioning that is temporary and changing, which leads to unreliably happy experiences because the reference we use is none other than a personal feeling of affection and therefore disconnected from the reality of the situation. Cultivating a state of mind imbued with kindness and compassion thus constitutes an important step. In the beginning, what we cultivate is only our own interpretation, but by coming back to the reference of the teaching, an understanding develops that is more than simply a mix of intuitions, emotional feelings, and personal wishes. Certainty becomes anchored within us without being manipulated by our own mental schemas. Our perception of situations and of others becomes clear. We develop enlightened mind in a genuine and less artificial way because it is founded on an understanding of the process of karma, most notably. The more genuine this state of mind becomes, the more space we obtain. Our point of reference changes, which influences our ordinary functioning. We adopt a new way of considering others and our state of mind evolves. A bodhisattva is no longer preoccupied by his own safety or unhappiness; his goal is to progress toward enlightenment to help others. This state of mind has the side effect of resolving difficult personal conditions and dissipating our own unhappiness.

## Becoming Free

The goal of the bodhisattva's path is to achieve enlightenment—in other words to ensure positive and happy conditions on a permanent basis. A bodhisattva seeks to completely liberate himself from unhappiness, which results in the accomplishment of Buddhahood. All of the conditions that we encounter, pleasant or unpleasant, are subject to change, to impermanence. Enlightenment is a state that can neither be modified nor altered. In general, we are ready to devote a great deal of time and energy to satisfy our desires or attain the goals we set; the downside is that this happiness never lasts. A bodhisattva's principal objective throughout his life is to focus on enlightenment in order to eradicate all forms of unhappiness. Due to the stability of this state, he can then be truly useful to others. Too often, we allow ourselves to be satisfied with an experience of immediate happiness, which is, in the long run, not satisfying. Therefore, we must develop awareness of the necessity of finding sustainable, definitive happiness.

It is a matter of carefully observing what makes sense for us. Certainly, there are many important things in life, but the idea is to adopt another way of thinking. The problem that hinders us from doing so can be summarized in one word: attachment. Even if we wish to become bodhisattvas, our overwhelming attachment to ourselves, to objects, and to other people holds us back and we do not manage to free ourselves from an unhappiness that, nonetheless, we do not want. We do not realize that attachment is the stumbling block that causes us to trip. Furthermore, attachment always comes with hopes and expectations that are often disappointed. It is important to remedy this ignorance through careful reflection and attentiveness to our contradictions if we wish to gain in independence and freedom. Regularly asking ourselves what is essential to us clarifies, step by step, the path that we wish to take and what it involves. Without this, we keep wishing to go south while taking a road that leads north, and we continue being surprised that we do not reach our destination!

The first step consists in being clear about what we want and the means to achieve it. If, in the image of the bodhisattvas, we wish to be free from unhappiness, we must start by observing where its causes lie. This introspective gaze causes our way of thinking to evolve. In this way, we begin down the path which leads to the desired destination. Enlightened mind is an essential element of this journey, for orienting our minds toward others means releasing the attachment that we hold toward ourselves.

The ordinary approach to happiness and the approach of the Dharma are entirely different. In general, we evolve based on our feelings and perceptions and we consider our way of living to be right. However, as soon as we reconsider this impression in connection with the notion of liberation, we see the flaws in this attitude that initially seemed natural. So long as we do not use liberation as our reference point, we think that unhappiness and hardship are the price we have to pay in life to enjoy a few pleasures and short-term well-being. As we begin to reflect on liberation, at first we are a bit confused because our habitual references are completely turned upside down, but this leads to a different perception and experience of situations that undermines our current way of living and perceiving things.

Understanding the causes of unhappiness is essential to giving rise to genuine enlightened mind. Furthermore, a rapid examination reveals that the pleasure or happiness of satisfying our hopes or expectations does not last and vanishes quickly. Becoming free from this in order to attain a stable state, enlightenment, thus seems relevant. We can then refocus our expectations on something truly useful: the development of enlightened mind. Kindness and compassion direct our vision toward others. Just like us, others create the conditions for their future unhappiness. This observation gives rise to the profound wish to help them, but to do so, we must develop our own capacities by committing to the path toward enlightenment. This is the aim of bodhisattvas. Their qualities are already present in us, but we do not have access to them because of various obscurations. It suffices to become aware of them and reveal them in their full expression. The conduct of bodhisattvas serves as a reference point so as not to follow a personal interpretation of enlightened mind. In addition, this reference acts as a reminder not to act impulsively based on the emotional occurrences that arise within our minds. In this way, we take care of ourselves. The mind develops a different way of thinking that reduces our self-centered thoughts.

As we have emphasized, only kindness and compassion lead to beneficial results in daily life. However, without proper discernment, they can also lead to making mistakes, and thus generate suffering despite the initial intention being beneficial. They must thus be accompanied by the practice of meditation. Enlightened mind and meditation make the ideal combination for progressing to enlightenment. Meditation alone does not allow for this. Indeed, without kindness and compassion, the discernment acquired through meditation does not necessarily lead to beneficial action. A person of great intelligence may create things that are very harmful for others. Meditation creates space in the mind that we ordinarily lack. It leads to developing our capacity to see things with greater accuracy and precision. This intelligence also allows us to better understand the teachings so we can apply them more appropriately.

Progressing toward enlightenment requires the correct dose of various elements, similar to gardening. Soil fertility, water, warmth, and the quality of the seeds all contribute to the proper development of a plant. Practicing enlightened mind separately from meditation—and vice versa—offers partial, but perfectly valid results. However, neither allows us to realize full enlightenment. So it is important to realize the necessity of acquiring greater clarity without neglecting the value of kindness and compassion. The same goes for cooking: preparing a single ingredient does not make for a very tasty dish. Good flavor results from a proper balance of several ingredients. In the beginning, an apprentice cook does not know how to prepare a recipe very well despite having all the ingredients—the result is not as appetizing as the same dish prepared by a chef. However, through continued effort and attempts, he improves. He knows his ingredients better, further masters their dosage and their preparation, and one day, the dish is perfect. The process is identical for the practice of Buddhism. First, we need to know which elements to combine. Then we have to work on our application in function of our own capacities and ability. Bringing everything together can at times be difficult, but it is a question of perseverance and patience, for there is no shortcut on the path to kindness and compassion.

Chapter 4

# The Practice of Meditation

## Prerequisites

Meditation is training the mind toward the goal of remaining concentrated without being distracted by thoughts. As previously explained, emotional and conceptual occurrences constantly arise in the mind. We have barely sat down when thoughts of the past and future assail us. The mind thus wanders along with this incessant flow. Meditation does not involve stopping thoughts (this is not feasible), but instead not being disturbed by their appearance in order to remain in mind's natural state. This training allows us to acquire a new habit: resting, without distraction, with mind itself.

For meditation practice as it is proposed in the Buddhist context to bring about its result, several conditions must be reunited in order to obtain a more profound result than simply relaxation of body and mind. The first involves knowing the functioning of our mind, as we have described it in the previous chapters. For meditation practice to be efficacious, it is important to familiarize ourselves with this process and its most subtle aspects by going beyond a superficial understanding.

Due to a clear comprehension of our functioning, the mechanism of our unhappiness also becomes clear in connection with the notion of karma. We realize that this unhappiness does not apply only to us, but, in fact, to everyone. Kindness and compassion thus enter the picture. These different points are not meant to be seen as separate themes; on the contrary, it is by bringing them together that a general understanding can emerge. These elements may seem self-evident, and understanding them superficially remains easy. However, pushing the analysis further causes questions to arise and challenges our fixed opinions on things. We then start to doubt our initial understanding.

Maintaining flexibility of mind is essential so as not to remain stuck in our own positions. Being endowed with intelligence, it is obvious that we will all acquire a basic degree of understanding. The point is not to remain blocked at this level, but to evolve toward a more subtle understanding based on refined observation. Then, questions arise and things become complicated in a way. When we put our opinions on the line, doubts appear. It is important to keep in mind that this is a natural process of evolution toward more profound understanding. It is necessary to put in effort to dissipate our hesitations by going back to the teachings about karma, the functioning of ordinary mind, the transitory nature of phenomena, etc. By combining this analysis with the practice of meditation, we succeed in clarifying our uncertainties and apprehending things according to a new perspective. This burgeoning understanding is founded on an experience different from our habitual one. Indeed, thanks to meditation, the mind gains clarity; in other words, it is capable of remaining in a state of awareness free from distractions. If we familiarize ourselves with this awareness, our perception becomes just, as it is free from emotional distractions and judgments.

We introduce the practice of meditation based on an understanding of our functioning, even a rudimentary one, and it acts like developing liquid in photographic processing. Due to the clarity meditation based on understanding allows us to develop, we apprehend this functioning in a much more precise and relevant way. To meditate means to familiarize oneself with our innate clarity of mind. Adventitious conditions distract us from this natural state and we slip into illusion and ignorance without even realizing it.

Illusion and ignorance are nothing other than our own perceptions colored by attachment and other emotional occurrences. Their strength carries away the mind and causes it to deviate from its own nature. Remaining with this dimension of clarity leads to no longer being subject to this influence, while remaining aware of the presence of attachment. We have not shed our obscurations, but we succeed in seeing the emotional occurrence and the process it triggers. Attachment in and of itself is not harmful; what counts is the kind of thinking that it leads to and the acts we carry out that activate the interdependent mechanisms connected to this first influence. A genuine comprehension of all this eradicates confusion and means that we can stay with clarity. We free ourselves from the hold of this emotional occurrence, all while becoming aware that this or that state is nothing other than our own minds.

## Our Natural State

When we meditate, the first thing is knowing who meditates. I meditate, so, what do this "I" and "self" look like? Is it solely our bodies that take a specific posture? The position of the body is only one factor and does not constitute the essence of meditation. It is thus the mind that meditates. While the body is the unification of tangible physical elements, mind has no perceptible form; mind is, by nature, the union of clarity and emptiness.

It is easy to observe the emotional and conceptual happenings arising within us and transforming according to the conditions and circumstances present. These occurrences are conditioned by a collection of factors that are perpetually changing. Thus, they cannot purport to be the natural, veritable, and stable state of the mind. Though our mind has no perceptible form or matter, it is not a void either. Something is indeed present. As it were, we experience all of this feeling that we are "ourselves" within the ephemeral, composite shells of our bodies. We have the capacity to perceive, to feel, to know, without necessarily being able to represent who perceives, feels, or knows.

In its natural state, mind is both clarity and emptiness at the same time. The term clarity means "precise and without confusion." The word "emptiness" does not refer to a vacuum, but to presence without representation: an innate quality of compassion, also called Buddha nature. If we succeed in dissipating the confusion that encompasses the mind, we can then remain with its essential nature. Clarity allows us to realize the causes of our confusion; we precisely understand that the mind takes wrong turns rather than remaining with its own nature. Instead of remaining with this clarity and emptiness, the mind grasps onto the occurrences triggered by inner and outer stimulus. These occurrences of attachment, rejection, judgment, and ignorance cause disturbances and cut us off from ourselves. The mind engenders its own confusion. Understanding this allows us to dissipate a great deal of difficulty and open new space. We are no longer as subject to our own emotions and we manage to maintain a distance from our ideas and feelings. By familiarizing ourselves with this quality of clarity, we see that the mind is lighter, less weighed down by useless occurrences, and over time we become capable of coming back to its original state. This is the premise of meditation, and, in contrast to what we might think, it is not a matter of slowing down but of clarifying.

According to the Buddha, the mind of all sentient beings is identical clarity and emptiness. In other words, we have the possibility to act in our present conditions and to evolve toward enlightenment. We are all endowed with qualities identical to those of a Buddha. They are simply obscured for the moment. Why do we not simply remain in this original state? Because the mind deludes itself. Due to an inner or outer circumstance, we grasp a feeling, which overtakes us, and we then lose all awareness or clarity. This obscuration has a snowball effect and combines with others like it to eventually produce a profound confusion and deeply anchored illusions. Mind is convinced of the reality and truth of its own biased perceptions that influence our decisions and actions.

Understanding this process is essential, for no one other than ourselves knows what happens in our minds and can remedy it. Having intellectual knowledge of this is a good starting point, but we must not stop there. Otherwise, we cannot put this knowledge to concrete use. Meditation is what allows us to profoundly integrate this understanding; it is a vector for evolution. Through training, everyone can come back to the original qualities of his mind. By remaining with these qualities of clarity and emptiness, of discernment and compassion, we do not engage with our various perceptions in the same way and we no longer let ourselves be influenced by them.

Understanding that our own essence is this Buddha nature and remaining in this dimension is not easy in the beginning. Our ideas and opinions often hinder our understanding. Similar to a research scientist, we engage in a process of methodical discovery where nothing is left to chance, but rather verified and tested. In the same way, it is necessary to observe and analyze what is happening in our minds. In the beginning, everything is fairly mixed up, which is normal. We acquire clarity and discernment gradually and without pressure. Over the course of our progress, we acquire a certainty that the mind cradles its own illusions and lets itself be diverted from wisdom to choose confusion.

Carrying out this introspection brings us closer to a state free from all confusion. Beings who have reached the end of their training have a much more balanced and peaceful state of mind. Due to this, these great bodhisattvas—who may be people on other spiritual paths, such as saints—have developed qualities superior to those of human norms. Though it is extraordinary, this result is nonetheless within our reach, as anyone can embrace this path. The master Gampopa was an ordinary doctor who was married with children. When he began practicing meditation after the death of his wife, he was more than forty years old. He became an extraordinary being and an exceptional teacher whose instructions we continue to follow today. There are no limiting conditions on meditation practice; it is available for everyone. Though its unfamiliarity may present difficulties at first, regular practice will eventually come easily through training. The result depends on correct application. If we practice the path appropriately, it is certain that we will obtain the intended result. It is enough to follow the methods proposed here, one of which is meditation.

Meditation prepares and trains our mind for this application. We have the option to stay on a theoretical level and continue intuitively in line with our own ideas; attaining a truly effective result remains uncertain, hazardous, and very time-consuming. This is tantamount to looking for a cure for a disease without any prior medical knowledge. The method of meditation supports the entire length of the path. By habituating the mind to spontaneous observation, meditation leads to identifying the emotional and conceptual process with greater and greater precision. Then, we clearly see that these occurrences come from the mind but do not constitute its true essence. Indeed, these occurrences appear and dissolve; they vary perpetually. Subject to multiple causes and conditions, they do not constitute a stable foundation, while the goal is to come back to mind's essential nature, to stability. This refers to its dimension of clarity and compassion. It is a question of remaining in this state, initially for a single moment, and then of prolonging this as long as possible.

## How to Meditate

You can begin by simply sitting down in a calm place. In the beginning, a calm environment is more supportive for focusing the mind. Next, follow a meditation method. Two options for meditation practice are possible: the meditation of mental calm and the meditation practices connected to the great bodhisattvas. These two possibilities, which lead to the same result, constitute two different styles of practice. For certain people it is more natural to focus on a simpler meditation, free from complex visualizations and recitation, while others prove more inclined to use various supports (visualizations, recitations of prayers or mantras, and other ritual aspects). The choice of one or another option is personal. It is important to emphasize that this is not a question of adaptation to the West, but of alternatives that traditionally exist within the Karma Kagyu lineage of Tibetan Buddhism.

Whatever the chosen method, meditation begins with proper posture. Shamar Rinpoche (1952–2014) explained the posture in this way[8]:

"It is best to sit up straight when you meditate. In case

---

8    Excerpt from *Boundless Awakening: The Heart of Buddhist Meditation*, Shamar Rinpoche, Bird of Paradise Press, Lexington, VA, 2013.

you sit on a chair, your feet should touch the ground and be parallel. If you are sitting cross legged on a mat, your legs can be completely crossed in the full lotus position, or alternatively they can be half-crossed with the right leg outside and the left inside. Generally, a person with longer legs sits on a higher cushion, but how high your seat is really depends on your physical proportions. It is important for your spine to be completely straight.

The stomach is slightly drawn inward, while the abdomen is very slightly pushed forward for balance. This keeps the central part of the body very straight. To enhance a straight central torso, your shoulders should also be balanced and straight.

The hands can be placed together in the posture of meditation. This means that the palms of the hands are face up, resting on your heels (if sitting in full lotus position), or resting in your lap a few finger widths below the navel, with the right hand on top of the left. This position further reinforces an upright and straight spine. Alternatively, you can rest your hands face down comfortably on your thighs towards the knees, taking care to keep the shoulders straight.

The neck should be slightly curved so that your chin is a little bit tucked in towards your chest. Your eyes are half open, looking ahead and cast slightly downward. Your mouth should neither be wide open nor pressed firmly closed. The lips should be relaxed in a very natural position. Breathing is mainly through the nose."

This posture encourages the meditative state, but if it is not possible to take this posture, that does not mean that you cannot meditate, for the principal element remains the mind. The posture is not a rule; it is a means to facilitate the relaxation of body and mind without giving in to torpor.

Let us discuss, firstly, the meditation of mental calm. This is a peaceful state of mind, in other words, without distractions. Distractions are not necessarily serious or violent; they can be quite subtle and benign. Whatever their intensity, all distractions share the common trait of creating disturbance, that is, an interruption, in the mind. These distractions are simply our own thoughts.

The meditation of mental calm thus consists of not wandering along with the thoughts that arise, but in being aware of their appearance and letting them dissolve without following them. With the help of a support, the meditator trains himself to develop a quality of attention and awareness. He tries to stay attentive so that the mind remains concentrated on its support and aware in terms of recognizing the emergence of a thought in order to come back to the object of focus as quickly as possible. Different types of supports exist; the most common is the breath. We simply place our mind on the natural rhythm of our inhalations and exhalations. It is possible to count the cycles of breath (three, seven, or twenty-one exhalations and inhalations) while trying not to be distracted from this count when a concept or an idea emerges. If we lose the count, we simply start from the beginning.

It is also possible to use an external support, like an object (such as a grain of rice or a stone) on which we place our gaze without tension. The procedure is similar: when a thought arises, we recognize it as quickly as possible and come back to our object of focus. We can also use an "inner" support by focusing on the Buddha's presence. This last option requires precise explanations and I recommend seeking them from a qualified teacher.

It is necessary to be patient and not get discouraged, as meditation is counter to our habits and the mind is always looking to satisfy or distract itself. For this method to yield its result, it requires effort and regular practice. In the beginning, we do not often manage to count more than two cycles of breath! We are often stressed about achieving the result. It is therefore important to specify that the essential point lies in the process itself. The term "meditate" in Tibetan means to familiarize oneself, to become habituated. Therefore, it is not a matter of putting pressure or trying to force ourselves, but of starting with short sessions of five minutes, for example, separated by breaks. Over the course of this training, we increase the length of the meditation or the number of breaths we count.

In this way, the mind frees itself little by little from the clutter of its thoughts. Through this exercise, we aim to remain with clarity as opposed to confusion, which means not letting the mind be interrupted and disturbed by the occurrences that arise within it. We cannot prevent thoughts from emerging—they arise constantly and naturally. In fact, thoughts are not the problem in and of themselves. It is their ceaseless continuity and what we make of it that is important, for often we let ourselves be carried away by them and lose our quality of presence. This instantaneous succession of ideas, concepts, and feelings takes up the whole of the mind. The method of meditation allows us to find space and clarity again.

The second option of meditation practice uses the support of great bodhisattvas through visualizations and recitations of mantras or prayers. These bodhisattvas personify enlightened qualities: compassion for the bodhisattva Avalokiteshvara, wisdom for the bodhisattva Manjushri, liberation for the bodhisattva Tara, etc. Once again, we make this choice based on personal affinity.

The methods known as "visualization" and recitation as well as the techniques of practice are specific to each bodhisattva and allow us to activate a connection with these great beings. The term "visualize" is often understood to mean "imagine a form," yet it is not a question of an exercise of mental or artistic projection, in which case any object could be imagined. Here, we are talking about the presence of the bodhisattvas, which means a precise appearance, which, though insubstantial, is the manifestation of qualities. The functioning of this type of practice can be compared to potential energy: energy is present all around us, but in order to harness and use it, we must put in place certain mechanisms.

The goal is to create a connection—also called blessing—that enriches our practice and allows us to acquire a better understanding of what mind is. This results in a certain stability. Over time, this meditation practice leads to developing the same qualities as the bodhisattvas to whom we connect. In the beginning, the link we create is somewhat artificial, but with time and progress, it truly manifests, as what we are cultivating concerns the same wishes as those of the bodhisattvas. Blessing can be compared to the sun, the heat and light of which allow for plants to grow. By connecting to a bodhisattva using the intermediary of a specific meditation practice, his blessing permeates us and contributes to maturing a certain clarity and qualities (compassion, wisdom, etc.) that become natural. We must apply ourselves to practice for evolution to occur. Otherwise, nothing will develop, like a seed sown in concrete. Indeed, the sprout of blessing will be present in us, but it will not be active and nothing will evolve on the level of mind. It is not a matter of some magical procedure, but of a process of maturation that requires the unification of several factors.

By concentrating on the presence of a great bodhisattva, the mind activates a connection that has an effect on its habits and ordinary concepts. The practitioner thus sees his functioning more precisely and develops his capacities. In this way, his mind is less subject to the influence of emotional and conceptual distractions. He gains discernment and naturally embraces the direction of a bodhisattva, in other words, enlightenment.


Whichever meditation we choose, regularity is the most important condition for the success of meditation practice. As for any sport or musical instrument, the result depends on the quality and regularity of training. If practice is regular, it generates a habit. Once the reflex is acquired, it is easier to continue in the same direction. Indeed, we must not stop at the first result achieved, but rather continue to pursue the path until we have reached our true, original potential. It is necessary to put in effort, though without forcing, for it is through training that the mind gains ever more clarity.

## The Results

The result of meditation practice corresponds to our original intention, the goal that we have set for ourselves. Let us go back to Shakyamuni Buddha. Why did he meditate? The Buddha was born a prince of the Sakya tribe. He excelled in all domains of worldly knowledge (philosophy, music, art, sports, etc.). Despite his royal position, which satisfied all his material and intellectual needs, he felt that something was missing. One day, he became aware of the unhappiness of sentient beings when he discovered sickness, old age, and death. Despite his riches and knowledge, he could only observe his own powerlessness against this unhappiness that we all experience. This realization became the motor for his quest: find a definitive remedy to this situation. After various fruitless spiritual experiments, the young Shakyamuni meditated. An understanding of the causes of this unhappiness emerged based on his meditation. He then cultivated this understanding until he reached full and perfect enlightenment.

In Buddhism, the practice of meditation has a precise goal: gain clarity and awareness in order to more correctly apprehend what we are as well as the world around us, with the goal of developing qualities such as discernment, kindness, and compassion. In this way, we free ourselves, and we likewise become able to help others.

Practice can bring two types of results connected to our motivation: absolute liberation from all unhappiness or a partial lessening of suffering that facilitates our daily existence.

Consider the first type of result: definitive liberation

from all unhappiness. In this case, the practice of meditation must be accompanied by study of the teachings. Meditation allows us to more profoundly integrate our initial intellectual understanding. The teachings we receive have a real and natural impact on our daily lives (our actions, choices, words, etc.). The combination of studying the teachings with meditation leads to developing our capacities. A clear mind understands more. Therefore, we act and communicate better as well. In addition, clarity likewise means fewer disturbances and distractions, and thus more space for ourselves, and especially for others.

Meditation practice consists in going through a process. It is important to have guidance and to speak with a qualified teacher who can respond to questions that will surely arise. If we practice meditation with discipline, it leads to a personal, individual experience of the functioning and the nature of our minds. We then directly recognize emotional and conceptual occurrences. When we accomplish this, the explanations of our minds are no longer just a nice story that someone else tells us or an opinion that we hold. We actualize the meaning. We clearly identify the causes of these occurrences, and we can thus alter them to free ourselves from confusion. The important thing is to create a habit of practice. In this way, over the course of our training we manage to remain for more and more time in this dimension of clarity. This is not yet enlightenment. However, the mind does succeed in approaching its basic nature without fabrication or artifice. At the end of this process, it is possible to become enlightened—in the image of practitioners at the time of the Buddha. This, then, is the absolute result.

Emotions no longer obscure the mind of a bodhisattva. This does not mean that they have been eradicated. Emotions are an integral part of our human functioning; without feeling, sensation, or emotion we would be things, objects. These occurrences thus remain present in the mind, but they no longer bring about harmful judgment. Anger is no longer a channel for unhappiness and desire no longer produces ephemeral joy. However, this does not mean that we fade into a bland and colorless dimension. On the contrary, we rejoice in a pleasant, stable state without complications or disturbances. The awareness acquired frees us from emotional and conceptual manipulations. We immediately recognize these occurrences and they naturally dissipate. We no longer identify others (family, friends, enemies, colleagues, etc.) as the cause of our problems. Instead they become the objects of our compassion. Indeed, we understand that we are all subject to the same functioning. The compassion that arises from this original state is therefore natural and without limit.

Another, more relative, form of result can also be obtained through meditation practice. By acquiring a more precise and genuine reference point for the functioning of our mind, our vision of others becomes gentler; we see that their reactions, like ours, are conditioned by their states of mind. Therefore, we become more patient and less judgmental toward them. The clarity and stability developed in meditation influence our way of being and allow us to act on the basis of something other than our ego. Rather, we base both our communication and our action on what is appropriate to the situation, which creates greater general harmony.

Family life is a savory mix of love, anger, and confrontation. The practice of meditation contributes to improving our relationships and appeasing conflict. The same goes for the professional milieu and, in general, our connections with all other human beings. When difficulties or unpleasant situations arise, we are less afraid, our minds are less agitated, and thus the quality of our presence is different. We communicate better and are a better source of support for others.

Furthermore, the clarity we obtain brings with it greater self-confidence. We realize that we can better manage the difficult emotional circumstances or situations that we encounter. We apprehend problems with greater precision and a more refined analysis. The discernment that comes from meditation allows us to more easily provide answers to our questions and difficulties. As we see here, meditation does not have the effect of eradicating the unpleasant situations with which we are confronted. However, it allows us to develop the qualities to face them more easily, notably due to a stable and anchored self-confidence that is not based on ego. Our decisions become more well-considered and less impulsive, which also reduces tension. These results constitute perceptible progress in our practice and provide veritable encouragement to continue on the path.

An openness thus appears, based on which we experience less aggressiveness and greater tolerance. Unconsciously, we continue to wish to stay in our comfort zone. If we perceive a lack of respect, we immediately feel displeased. Meditation acts on this feeling and leaves space for another way to envisage the situation. It is not a question of sacrifice, but of changing our point of view to adopt that of the other person and to try to understand. We gain perspective on the situations in which we find ourselves and this dissipates irritation. This is how our relationships with our family, friends, and colleagues progressively simplify and become more fluid with time. By being less focused on our personal perception, we become more available for others.

These so called relative results are not negligible. In this way, any individual who wishes to improve his life conditions through serious practice but who does not necessarily have the goal of obtaining enlightenment can reap great benefits from meditation. It is important to practice in accordance with our capacities and abilities of the moment without falling into one extreme or another. Furthermore, the result that we wish to realize can also evolve along the path and shift from the relative to the absolute.

At this stage, it seems important to specify that the experiences that come from meditation practice have little in common with fantastical visions, divine light shows, or other miracles. The nearly imperceptible change in our habits constitutes the veritable result. We naturally put to work the causes for lasting happiness and, without forcing, give up the causes that lead to unhappiness. Only the regular repetition of this exercise leads to this genuine result.

## Complements to Meditation

Good preparation in advance is required for those who wish to meditate in order to definitively free themselves from unhappiness and progress toward enlightenment with the motivation of a bodhisattva. This preparation consists of studying the teachings and their application, as explained in the previous chapters. This is what takes meditation to another level. Regularity of practice is also an essential ingredient.

One text called *Placing the Focus Closest to Four [Objects]*, which we discussed earlier in connection with attachment, is particularly useful. Directly issued from the sutras, this teaching invites us to investigate the nature of the physical body, sensations, mind, and phenomena. It describes reality as it is. An understanding of this subject changes our way of connecting with life: we naturally move toward detachment. We then accept all situations that we encounter as they are. Whether we live in a fantastically verdant landscape or suddenly find ourselves in an arid locale filled with rocks and stones no longer has any importance, for we are no longer as attached to physical aspect. Mind remains close with its own nature.

Detachment is not to be understood as rejection or indifference but as an understanding of reality that orients us toward what is essential.

This type of teaching nurtures our practice, while meditation itself refines our initial understanding; the two are mutually beneficial. Connecting study of the teachings and meditation practice contributes to the maturation of the different types of discernment based on listening, reflecting, and meditating. It is in this way that we move closer to our full potential in order to unveil it, as did the great bodhisattvas.

## What About Compassion?

Gaining clarity of mind or, in other words, intelligence,

is not a measure of benefit. Indeed, the people who cause the most harm in the world are often very intelligent. The result of meditation, particularly mental calm, can thus be used for unfortunate ends. One element is crucial to ensure that we go in the right direction: compassion. It is the guiding light that orients clarity of mind in a beneficial direction.

If we protect our minds from the ego game of emotions, we have more concern for others and for ourselves. We thus act in a more beneficial way (which also has a positive influence on our karmic conditions). Kindness and compassion bring us closer to others and distance us from inflexibility. They act like the roots of a tree; a tree can grow quite tall, but if its roots are not stably anchored, it can easily topple. The same goes for the result of meditation practice. If the foundation is not solid, it will not last.

In the beginning, compassion is partial and colored by personal feeling, but it progressively becomes genuine and equal toward all.

The ultimate goal of Buddhist practice is the attainment of enlightenment. This is the direction that orients our practice. Accomplishing this final step remains difficult, but it is quite possible. Several months or years of practice will not be enough; we must count on longer than that. At the same time, another alternative result is more within our reach: approaching the accomplishment of the great saints or bodhisattvas.

A true bodhisattva is not prisoner of the various life conditions that all beings encounter. The only difficulty that can create obstacles lies in our deeply rooted habits, which go in the opposite direction of what we seek on the path. Meditation practice remedies this, but remains incomplete if we do not incarnate the way of being and acting of the bodhisattvas.

Chapter 5

# Accomplishing Benefit

**Altruistic Thought in Action**

A bodhisattva's way of thinking and acting is based solely on kindness and compassion. His only motivation is to be useful to others. All ordinary beings experience unhappiness. Bodhisattvas, having freed themselves from this experience, wish to help others liberate themselves from it. By following their example of how to act and how to consider situations, we develop our capacities in order to become bodhisattvas in our own right. It is not possible to exist without doing anything; we act in every instant. The goal is thus to orient the mind and to direct our actions toward what is beneficial.

In daily life, a bodhisattva's way of thinking and acting goes against that of ordinary human beings. This seems strange at first glance, but let us come back to our basic functioning to understand better. As we described in greater detail in the preceding chapters, when a thought arises in the mind, an impulsive feeling comes with it that influences our actions. This is how our typical way of functioning continuously leads to greater unhappiness. However, as this is our natural functioning, we do not think about questioning it nor modifying our perspective.

A bodhisattva is also a human being, but he apprehends things according to another point of view: that of others. In this way, his mode of being proves considerably more perfect than our own. Applying enlightened mind does not mean following a bunch of rules. Instead, it refers to developing understanding so that we are able to embody the qualities of enlightened mind. Based on the bodhisattvas' examples of conduct and concrete situations, we try to apply the same state of mind in relation with our own capacities, without forcing anything. Anyone who wishes to attain the perfection of the bodhisattvas must simply begin where he is. Step by step evolution is a guarantee of progress without regression or giving up. Over the course of the path, our way of seeing, but also our expectations and our understanding changes. We become more beneficial for others. Based on this, we contribute to establishing a peaceful state of mind and developing greater harmony in our relationships.

Application in daily life quickly gives rise to the initial results, which encourage us to continue. We witness the good that this brings about for others and for ourselves. Following the perfect conduct of the bodhisattvas to the letter is not immediately within our reach, but neither is it simply a myth. It is certain that one day we will realize this perfection if we train with sincerity.

Change can only occur through practical application of this mind training.

Here, we directly connect the method with daily life. The goal is to use every situation to develop our minds—a practice that goes against our habits. Indeed, when facing difficulties, mistakes, or unkindness, our primary reflex is to identify who is responsible in order to reveal the truth of the situation. A bodhisattva does not react this way; he focuses on another goal.

In general, the source of all beings' suffering is the desire for self-centered happiness. Indeed, if we are honest, we will realize that the cause of our unhappiness comes from being too focused on ourselves. Turning this habit around is not easy.

A bodhisattva does not experience any unhappiness because he is not fixated on himself, but instead focused on others. Consider this example of the difference between a bodhisattva and an ordinary being. When an ordinary being acquires a new property, his first reflex is often to put up a fence around his land to protect himself from thieves, animals, and all other potential damage that could occur. We build barriers because we are thinking of ourselves. A bodhisattva or a Buddha does not need to put walls up around himself. He is naturally close to other beings without fear or worry. One of the outcomes of kindness and compassion is that we no longer discriminate against others. Because we have not yet sufficiently developed this quality, ordinary beings experience suffering.

The principal practice of bodhisattvas for developing kindness and compassion is that of exchanging self for others. A bodhisattva gives all that is positive and beneficial to others and takes on all that is harmful and difficult himself. This is the true condition and way of life of authentic bodhisattvas. In our case, we use this principle to train concretely in daily life in order to change our states of mind.

This exchange is not a sacrifice we make in order to receive a reward. Considering the training in this way does not allow for evolution and creates tensions that often lead to abandoning the path. The proposed approach only fully functions based on understanding the condition of beings. This is why the preparation explained in the previous chapters is necessary. It is not enough to simply repeat over and over that ignorance obscures the minds of beings and influences their way of acting. We must truly take the measure of this reality. The strength of this awareness allows us to apply the bodhisattvas' training. The exercise of exchanging self for others, described in detail in the following section, begins with benign situations and progresses through difficult circumstances. As this is not our natural impulse, it requires effort in the beginning.

The goal of training ourselves to act like bodhisattvas is to reveal our own potential. If we do so, at the end of the path we are truly useful to others and capable of reducing their suffering.

## Taking Disturbances as the Path

In 17th century Tibet, there lived a great bodhisattva by the name of Choying Dorje, the 10th Karmapa. Numerous political difficulties troubled the roof of the world at this time. As the head of the Karma Kagyu school of Tibetan Buddhism, Karmapa Choying Dorje was, of course, involved in these historical issues. At a certain point, the opposition overthrew him and ran him out of the country. His entourage and many of his disciples wanted to support him and fight to reveal the truth, but he prevented them from doing so. He did not want people to commit negative acts so that he could reclaim his rightful position. The 10ᵗʰ Karmapa became a beggar who wandered barefoot like a vagrant. Those who met and recognized him wished to help him. Though he accepted food and clothes, he categorically refused any violence in the name of his reputation. He regularly lost his possessions to bandits, but he always retained equanimity of mind. He never felt sorry for himself or resented those who stole from him. On the contrary, he dedicated his lost belongings to his assailants and profoundly rejoiced that he was able to be of service to them. This leniency is not a sign of moral weakness; it is the practice of bodhisattvas. The 10ᵗʰ Karmapa also habitually redistributed the offerings that he received without preference or discrimination. His sole wish and his sole line of conduct were those of enlightened mind, regardless of the cost to himself.

It is very unlikely that we would act the same way in an identical situation. This conduct may seem strange, shocking even. It is important to keep in mind that a bodhisattva's wish is to accomplish the benefit of others and to refrain from harming them under any circumstances. The possession of material wealth versus a life of total poverty does not influence their state of mind. In our case, we remain attached to our possessions and our person. Thus, it is difficult to rejoice for the thief who strips us of our cherished belongings. If a pickpocket steals something from us, our immediate reaction is anger. Not giving in to this anger is tricky. The training consists in maintaining presence of mind without giving in to the impulse of the moment. It is not a matter of forcing, but of simply beginning with what occurs in our minds. Successful and genuine application in daily life has two benefits. Firstly, this reduces our own unhappiness, as anger is not a pleasant sensation. Secondly, we directly alleviate the karmic consequence of the harmful action of the thief. In fact, if we rejoice that the object he stole from us may be useful to him, the action committed no longer constitutes a theft on his part but a gift on ours. The importance lies in doing so with conviction.

The training is the same if we are accused of a wrong we did not commit. A bodhisattva accepts his fate without seeking to reveal the truth. To do so would lead to the accusation of another, and a bodhisattva's commitment is to take on the causes of every harmful act in order to alleviate the suffering of beings. An ordinary attitude involves trying to prove the truth because "it's not fair!" This is exactly the type of reaction that perpetuates unhappiness. Instead, we must work on our states of mind and not on the external situation. Authentic compassion comes with greater discernment. We develop clear perception of what is happening, and this understanding leads us beyond our own vision of things. We do not analyze situations based on external facts, but instead, we ask the appropriate questions based on our goal— becoming a bodhisattva. Then, true compassion arises, and this compassion orients our reaction. Indeed, we become aware of the condition of others and we perceive that their actions stem from their states of mind and that they create the causes of their own future un-happiness. This understanding dissipates all anger and opens the way for compassion.

Likewise, when we are the target of rumors or defa-mation, the practice of bodhisattvas consists in under-standing the ignorance of those behind the falsehoods. We do not seek vengeance, nor do we give in to the dis-turbance such situations can create in our minds. We are aware of the unpleasant occurrences arising in our minds, and we do not succumb to them. Instead, we choose to adopt an unusual line of conduct; we kindly praise the qualities of our aggressors.

If someone reveals our flaws or insults us in public, we do not reject the situation, and we consider the hos-tile person to be a friend who wishes us well. We use the experience to improve ourselves and to progress along the path. The same goes for a person who disdains us or denigrates our work out of pride.

If a person we have taken care of in the past—even raised as our own child—turns against us, accuses us, or betrays us, we do not cultivate anger or desire for ven-geance. Instead, we fortify our kindness, like a mother toward a sick child.

All of these points relate directly to our emotional relationships with others and offer opportunities to live based on the attitude of enlightened mind.

When faced with poverty or illness, we may sink into suffering. A bodhisattva's attitude involves not be-coming discouraged or affected by this unhappiness. Instead, a bodhisattva pursues his commitment: trans-forming these difficulties into the path toward enlightenment by taking on the negative karma of beings while giving them all that is beneficial. Indeed, a bodhisattva has developed the quality of mind that does not experience either pride or discouragement. Fully concerned with his commitment to help other beings, he does not consider himself to be important. His conduct is sincere and spontaneous. Emotional occurrences no longer veil his mind; he is clearly aware of even the most minute causes and conditions in each situation that he encounters.

This level of achievement signifies that one has attained a form of fulfillment. Free from unhappiness, life is pleasant. We manage difficulties more easily. The causes of fear, worry, rejection, and anger are not active in the mind. We consider all situations and phenomena with equanimity.

Harmful thoughts always disturb an ordinary mind because it cannot identify their origin. This leads to a lot of confusion and an incorrect vision of things. In terms of pleasant thoughts, we immediately try to grasp them and preserve them; we do not accept that they are fleeting. Bodhisattvas see this identical functioning in all beings. Based on this vision, they generate unlimited compassion. They know that ignorance and harmful acts are the cause of the suffering of all beings.

We may naturally and spontaneously accept the idea of enlightened mind, but its application remains tricky. Therefore, it is important to train progressively, so that we do not become discouraged and give up. Wishing prayers also support this exercise. Certain great bodhisattvas expressed specific aspirations for developing enlightened mind, like the bodhisattvas Samantabhadra and Shantideva. Reading and repeating these wishes anchors their meaning in the mind. In the beginning, saying, "May the poor and destitute find wealth, the haggard and careworn, joy. May confidence relieve those in despair and bring them steadfastness and every excellence. May every being ailing with disease be freed at once from every malady. May all the sickness that afflicts the living be instantly and permanently healed[9]," is not necessarily natural. Getting used to this habituates us to seeing things in a different way and affects our conduct. Regularly expressing these aspirations reinforces our commitment to the path of kindness and compassion and leaves an imprint of enlightened mind. Little by little, we grasp the signification and our minds connect to the meaning of the words. We then become capable of expressing it through beneficial acts.

Helping others seems normal. However, if we honestly examine our own state of mind, we will realize that our wish to help others often hides an expectation (for recognition, for something in return, etc.) and if we gain nothing from our action then our motivation weakens. The exercise consists in first generating a habit—beginning with small daily actions without any hope for recompense. Doing so constantly creates a tendency that goes solidly in the direction of enlightenment. Often, in daily life the slightest disappointed expectation or dissatisfaction easily disconnects us from this orientation and we give in to discontent and frustration. If our irritation persists, it increases and we cut ourselves off from

---

9   Quotation from Shantideva, *The Way of the Bodhisattva*: A Translation of the Bodhicharyāvatāra, Shambala Publications, Inc., Boston, Massachusetts, 1997.

others. All unpleasant and unhappy conditions come from being overly focused on ourselves. The practice of exchanging self for others as we described it here remedies this and uproots the seeds of future unhappiness. This precise understanding of our functioning as well as the clarity obtained through meditation constitute a solid foundation for this training and begin the process of transformation.

It is useful to have a reference point that acts as a reminder of the direction we wish to take. Therefore, remember to keep the mind relaxed, whatever the circumstances. It is not about relaxation in terms of leisure, but rather relaxing the mind as soon as we see that certain causes and conditions have created tension. A relaxed mind does not give in to the panic of predominant emotional occurrences and naturally remembers what to apply to work with the situation at hand.

## Civilizing Our Minds

A good mastery of the mind is a key point in this training. This means civilizing the mind's rebellious habit of following the slightest emotional occurrences. We must implement this discipline gradually; forcing change does not last. If we do not tame our inner passions, outer difficulties only multiply.

A bodhisattva overcomes his anger through kindness and compassion. Because he sees all situations clearly, there is no longer any cause for this emotion to arise. We particularly emphasize anger here because it is one of the principal causes that triggers harmful actions.

In the same way that a bodhisattva does not give in to anger, he likewise goes beyond his personal preferences.

He does not entertain them because he knows that the more one succumbs to pleasure, the greater desire becomes. Pleasure is like saltwater; the more we drink, the thirstier we get and that thirst remains unquenchable. As soon as we have fulfilled one desire, we go in search of a new satisfaction. Cultivating this process creates endless attachment and limitless unhappiness.

Going beyond what brings us pleasure does not mean contenting oneself with suffering. This process instead concerns offering pleasant things to others rather than keeping them for ourselves. This aspect of a bodhisattva's conduct is part of intelligent generosity. If he notices that someone needs something in his possession, he offers it joyfully, whatever its value.

We act according to dualistic functioning. If we find something agreeable, we wish to acquire it no matter what, and if we do not like something, we want to get rid of it as quickly as possible. Every situation provokes an emotional reaction. This reaction colors the mind as well as the action or words that directly follow. The interdependence of our states of mind and our actions results in the genesis of unhappiness in all its forms.

Observing the way we use our time is an important part of the practice of bodhisattvas. We think and act in every moment. Considering what we do allows us to become more aware of what is happening and to adapt our state of mind and our conduct if needed. If we do not engage in this reflection, the days and months pass without our knowing what we are actually putting in place for our future—what seeds we are planting and what fruit we will harvest. Some kind of self-concern generally motivates our words and actions: pride in some cases, jealousy in others. Understanding this changes our perception and the quality of our communication. Even if our actions are not very harmful, we develop a habit and these seemingly insignificant negativities accumulate, often without our realizing it.

## The Six Perfections

We can summarize the previously described attitude of bodhisattvas in six types of training, called the six perfections: generosity, ethical attitude, patience, joyful effort, meditation, and discernment. It is necessary to cultivate the six perfections in the mind and also to apply them concretely.

A bodhisattva naturally practices generosity. Free from all attachment, he acts solely based on the needs of others. The generosity in question refers to acting in accordance with what is needed and using all of our available qualities and capacities to be of service to others. Giving refers not only to providing material wealth but also to helping and supporting others—to offering what is needed (time, a thoughtful ear, etc.). It is the complete opposite of maintaining our distance and staying in our comfort zone. Abbé Pierre[10] is a good example of perfect generosity. This quality can take different forms. It is not reserved to the wealthy, but begins with the question, "How can I be useful to others?" Practicing generosity on our level—without expecting a reward—sets in motion a beneficial karmic process for others and

---

10   Translator's note: Abbé Pierre (1912–2007) is a well-known French cultural icon. He was a French Catholic priest and the founder of the Emmaus movement, which aims to help the poor and homeless.

ourselves. A first act of generosity acts as a seed, which ripens into a beneficial fruit, and thus generates a dynamic of beneficial action. This attitude of sharing and openness closes the door to unhappiness.

Good conduct or ethical action signifies acting without committing harmful acts. In connection with generous action, ethical conduct allows us to move in a beneficial direction. It guarantees that an action has the proper motivation and orientation. Indeed, an act can be generous without being beneficial, such as the act of giving weapons. Positive ethic thus means maintaining the direction of enlightened mind.

Patience is the third perfection and refers to confronting difficulties without giving up or acting harmfully. In addition to this, when a bodhisattva faces anyone hostile or harmful to himself, he does not allow his mind to consider the person an enemy or to develop resentment. He simply exercises patience without reacting impulsively or negatively, which neutralizes anger.

The notion of joyful effort is part of a bodhisattva's quality of patience. He does not accept unfortunate situations without reacting. He is always eager to be of benefit. Whatever the difficulty or the length of the task, he works tirelessly without procrastinating what needs to be done. Joyful effort also implies not becoming discouraged and persevering instead. This quality is an excellent remedy for laziness.

Meditation is the element that causes the previous four

qualities to be effective. However, in the context of the perfections, this point does not refer to training in meditation, but rather to the result. A bodhisattva with extensive meditation experience remains in a state of mind free from distraction and disturbance. This complete meditative absorption eradicates the seeds of obscuration.

The combination of the first five perfections allows one to develop a powerful potential, that of perfect discernment. Without this clear understanding, we cannot reach enlightenment. Perfect discernment refers to an infallible intelligence, what one could call a perfect mind—a mind completely free of confusion and ignorance. This complete discernment leads beyond unhappiness. We then perceive reality as it is, both in terms of its nature and the diversity of its manifestation. The seeds of unhappiness no longer arise. The concepts of a subject that acts, an action, and an object of action—the basis for duality and unhappiness—dissipate. All that remains is a clear understanding of reality, which becomes the impetus for enlightened activity for the benefit of beings.

Applying these six qualities equates with living in total perfection. The goal is not to devote just a few hours a day or a certain amount of time we have set aside to this application. The bodhisattvas incarnate this perfection in every moment, without vacation or time off. However, we do not yet possess these qualities, but they indicate the direction we wish to follow. It is enough for us to encourage ourselves and to begin to put the qualities into practice according to our present capacities and without becoming discouraged. Doing our best to apply these six perfections allows us to progress along the path.

We do not need a particular context to begin applying the qualities; we can do so anywhere. On our meditation cushion, they act as a reminder. When we interact with others, we concretely put them to the test. All the situations that we encounter in life are opportunities to try to apply enlightened mind. The six perfections are examples of the direction to follow to ensure that we do not get lost. These references help us distinguish what is beneficial from what is harmful.

At times this reality seems so distant from our own lives that it can be tempting to think that all this is just a charming legend. However, this is not the case! Reading biographies of great bodhisattvas like the 10th Karmapa prove the veracity of these explanations. I myself witnessed this perfection in the form of the 16th Karmapa (1924 1981). When he lived in Rumtek, in Northeast India, he woke up at four-thirty in the morning every day and rarely went to bed before midnight. He consecrated every minute of his time to others. Without tension or pressure, he simply accomplished what was required. Often this meant receiving visitors—sometimes people who had travelled hundreds or thousands of miles to meet him and make a request. Whether the person was a ruler or a local farmer, he maintained the same quality of attention and listening as he tried to best respond to their questions and appeals. Sometimes, a family would come to ask for rituals for a deceased loved one. The Karmapa immediately took it upon himself to carry out extensive practices for the deceased. In addition to giving audiences, he was responsible for the education of

young teachers and took the time to transmit the teachings to them and to ensure that they understood the
words and their meaning correctly. As the lineage hold-
er of the Karma Kagyu, he verified that the programs of
study were authentic, the rituals accomplished properly,
and the conditions for practice respected. He also travelled around the world to respond to the requests made
of him. He never held back for a single moment. Just like
the bodhisattvas, he offered his support constantly and
without judgment. Sickness and fatigue never phased
him.

These great bodhisattvas are extraordinary beings
whose role is simple: be useful to sentient beings and
offer them what they need without criticism or judgment. Their activity comes from a spontaneous and sincere motivation and enthusiasm toward others that is
neither impulsive nor based on attachment. Though we
have not yet attained this level of perfection, we can still
try to support and help each other, to be attentive, and
to improve our listening, etc. Through regular training,
we can develop not only good habits but good karmic
conditions. Accumulating beneficial actions reduces
negative karma and contributes to preparing for a good
future destiny. In this way, we can attain positive life
conditions connected to the tendencies of enlightened
mind that we have developed in the previous life. Due
to this connection, we can once again meet with advan-
tageous circumstances to continue our progress on the
path of enlightened mind. Life after life, we can advance
in this way until we reach enlightenment.

This way of life requires effort and we can be lazy at
times. Understanding the process of development allows for more diligent application.

## Chapter 6
# Not Causing Harm

Another aspect of a bodhisattva's commitment is not committing harmful actions. He makes an effort not to be a source of negativity for two reasons: for himself and for others. In the same way that he consecrates himself to helping beings, he also takes care not to harm them, whatever he does. He constantly examines his state of mind and makes sure not to let the kindness and compassion he has developed diminish.

## Examining Our States of Mind

In daily life, we act in every moment. At times, we do so consciously, at others we do so without really paying attention to what we say or do, and at yet other times, we act in total ignorance. The fact is, in general we do not reflect enough on the thoughts that arise in our minds and the acts that we carry out. Due to this carelessness, we create the causes for our own unhappiness.

The mind allows for perception; in other words, it allows us to know. As explained in the previous chapters, our perceptions do not remain neutral. They quickly engender feelings (pleasant, unpleasant, or undefined) that provoke judgments and reactions (attraction, rejection, or indifference). All of this conditions our words and actions. We are so habituated to this mechanism that it takes place without our even noticing. It governs our cognition and all of our perceptions. Despite this, we are under the illusion that we act independently and make our own decisions.

Bodhisattvas have clearly identified this human functioning, and thus guard themselves against it by frequently inspecting what occurs within their minds. Indeed, knowing this mechanism in detail is a good foundation, but this alone does not interrupt the process. We easily fall victim to our habits and cause harm without even noticing. Remedying this is a matter of constantly observing what is happening within us and taking care that our emotional reactions do not develop into beliefs that we no longer question. This development of unquestioned beliefs is a deeply rooted habit. It accompanies all our movements and actions—from the most insignificant to the most important—and shapes those to come.

A good understanding of the mechanism of cause and effect is essential on the path to developing authentic kindness and compassion. The majority of people do not wish to cause harm and take no pleasure in it. In general, everyone wants to be good. However, we sometimes think we are doing something positive, but the outcome of our action is the opposite of what was intended. This happens based on a partial or superficial understanding of karma. A bodhisattva's attitude requires a sharp and disciplined observation of the mind's emotional occurrences. Though it is impossible to stop them, we can, however, recognize them with precision and be aware of their tricks to avoid getting caught up in them. This is how bodhisattvas undo their own illusion. This process requires being very honest with ourselves and accepting our faults. If we do not recognize our flaws, we cannot move past them and progress. If we do not, for example, admit the seed of subtle jealousy that influences a word or action, we risk causing harm, all while maintaining the appearance of a good practitioner.

What we say and our criticisms of others—whether or not they are founded—make up another aspect of harmful action. Complaints and criticism are part of human nature, whatever form they take. Because they nurture the emotional occurrences that obscure the mind and lead to losing the clarity that we seek to cultivate, bodhisattvas take care not to give in to criticism and complaining even though they are normal habits. Some critique is necessary and legitimate. The approach here is not about the act itself but the act in terms of its origin and what it triggers within us and others.

Consider the natural process of criticism. If we are with a person who is criticizing someone, we can observe that we willingly join in and even encourage the discussion. Likewise, if we are complaining, and someone affirms what we express, we feel some kind of satisfaction and complicity. Therefore, we must try to precisely identify the feeling that provokes criticism. It is connected to the idea of a self that wants to exist, to be heard, etc. Most of the time, we will see that we have simply followed this feeling without being aware of it. This feeling leads to various judgments and opinions that succeed one another, bring about yet others, and generally carry the mind along in their wake. They mark our minds with a counterproductive tendency. They carry us further from a beneficial state of mind and create obstacles to peace and harmony, from within our families to a much larger scale. This process is simply the ordinary mechanism of emotion—that of impulsively reacting to the conditions we encounter. It limits the development of mind's capacities. We lose the qualities we have acquired and stray from our goal—the direction of enlightened mind.

The mind is like a medicinal plant; if we use it correctly, it can remedy various ills and possesses great virtues. However, if we are not aware of its exact properties, it can act as a poison. The dimension of clarity and compassion is simultaneous with the possibility of ignorance. Being aware of the habitual processes of our minds allows us to remain with the clear and compassionate aspect of mind. Otherwise, we leave the door open for ignorance.

Examining what is happening within us becomes a personal experience. We directly observe the emotional cogs and switches. Then, we are able to truly live without being slaves to our own manipulation. This also permits us to clarify our views and attitudes. Carrying out such analysis is particularly relevant in our era, as we are constantly bombarded with information—rumors, propaganda, and advertising—that is often unreliable.

Acquiring this awareness prevents us from becoming "sheep."

The intention is neither to vilify critique, nor to feel guilty when we are caught in the act. This is pointless. The idea is to consider all of the ramifications of our views, words, and actions in order not to harm ourselves and others. If we understand how to manage the impulse to criticize, we will be able to apply this skill in other circumstances. If we no longer fall prey to the illusion created by the occurrences in our minds, we will acquire a better vision of reality.

## Preserving the Qualities Developed

A bodhisattva's conduct comes directly from the example of the Buddha as well as from study, contemplation, and meditation based on the Buddha's teaching. These practices allow us to acquire the discernment associated with each one. However, certain conditions can undermine the qualities we develop. A bodhisattva in training is still developing, which means that he has not yet anchored the qualities within himself. Like a child learning to walk who takes unsteady steps, he may potentially trip and fall. Due to our dualistic vision, we have a desire to be right and a wish to keep things for ourselves, which pushes us into competitiveness and vying for our own benefit. Based on this tendency, we incessantly create the conditions that nurture rivalry and seeking our own gain. This process undermines the qualities we may have acquired.

How does a bodhisattva deal with this? He avoids duality. This might seem like a very good idea, but we quickly reach a stumbling block. How do we do this? Avoiding the conditions of duality means remaining free from attachment. A bodhisattva lives completely free from self-interested discrimination. He does not differentiate between the outcome of his own gain or loss, nor his own benefit or harm. He may find himself the target of others' ill will, but he does not become angry or cultivate resentment. Likewise, if he receives special attention, he does not cling to it. His mind remains even and impartial. Thus, he maintains much more genuine relationships with people, and he relates more authentically to his surroundings.

As for us, we naturally enjoy what benefits or pleases us. We immediately become attached to pleasant physical or mental sensations, which leads us to seek them out exclusively. Whenever we encounter an unpleasant sensation or situation, we automatically reject it. This clinging to our preferences becomes a habit that we constantly cultivate, and it takes up most of our time and energy. We divide the world into three categories: what we want, what we want to avoid, and that to which we are indifferent. All of our problems stem from these self-centered divisions that condition our feelings and actions. The time and energy we devote to seeking our own satisfaction takes up a lot of space in our minds, and we easily lose sight of what is essential. Inevitably, our training in enlightened mind suffers.

A bodhisattva does not categorize beings. He directs his compassion equally toward those who cause harm and those who devote themselves to virtue—as much to the hunter as to his prey. His view does not fluctuate according to the situation as he no longer experiences the dualistic functioning of clinging and rejection. His activity for others consists, on the one hand, of offering help, and, on the other, of not causing harm. This second part has two aspects: not hurting others and also not creating disturbances in their minds. Due to his precise understanding of the mechanism of karma, a bodhisattva is extremely vigilant not to create opportunities for others to react negatively and sow seeds that will bring them unhappiness.

Thus, bodhisattvas make an effort not to distress others with harsh or hurtful words that can lead to confusion and damage enlightened mind.

The words we say can make the person with whom we are speaking angry. This emotional occurrence leaves an imprint in the person's mind. According to the intensity of the feeling, the circumstances, and the states of mind that develop from this imprint, it can degenerate and become a truly difficult experience.

If we do not take care, dandelion seeds carelessly thrown on a rock can sprout when the wind brings them soil and the rain waters them. The dandelion we wanted to get out of our garden can once more overtake it. Karma functions the same way. We never know ahead of time which causes or conditions will activate an imprint in the mind. Even a tiny seed can grow to become a giant tree.

The goal of coming back to this subject again and again is not for us to take up a radical and oversimplified approach to karma. It is not helpful to jump to the conclusion that every slight discomfort is a karmic result. The point is to understand the complexity of the process for ourselves and for others and to see how the two interact.

Part of the difficulty lies in the fact that we cannot perceive the mechanism of karma directly. Because it is not easily apparent to us, we do not truly recognize its importance. In this way, karma is similar to radioactivity. People remain in places where they are exposed to radioactive waves because they do not personally feel any change in their environment. Eventually, they become seriously ill, but once the result is present, it is already too late.

It is difficult to conduct ourselves in a way that is completely pure every day. However, if we are very aware of the karmic mechanism, we can identify the feelings that motivate an act and choose not to follow them. If we do not take others into consideration in our approach, we simply continue to cultivate the process of dissatisfaction without realizing we are doing so. This is why bodhisattvas make an effort not to create disturbances for others. In order to do so, they take great care of their own states of mind.

It does not help to try and force ourselves to constantly think about others. Instead, we can focus on our states of mind and on cultivating openness toward others. If we are not subject to outer circumstances, sincerity alone allows us to naturally remain with this way of being. But of course, our way of communicating or presenting things depends on the situation—in other words, the individuals present.

Taking care of our states of mind and developing greater openness generates more tolerance toward others. Indeed, how can we reproach them for acting according to a way of functioning that we share? With this understanding, compassion arises that neither judges nor discriminates. We become able to adjust our ethic and our conduct (particularly by being more patient), which has an effect on our daily lives. Our lives take a positive direction and we face fewer disturbances. This synergy of our state of mind and our circumstances creates a generally positive dynamic that naturally leads us to cause less harm.

Chapter 7

# The Nature of Phenomena

In the chapter on meditation, we discussed the nature of mind. It is useful to come back to this topic in greater detail and to consider all phenomena. Developing familiarity with these notions offers precious keys for the application of a bodhisattva's conduct.

## The Nature of Mind

It is tempting to think that the brain, the heart, or the body is the source of mind, but this is not the case. The natural state of mind of all beings is clarity and emptiness. Let us look at these terms more closely. We easily connect the term "emptiness" with some sort of vacuum, like an empty house waiting for a new tenant to arrive or simply an absence of existence. Neither of these two examples applies to the mind. In regards to the word "clarity," this does not refer to luminosity. What, then, makes up the mind? It is a collection of qualities:

a presence without form or substance that is pure intelligence, clarity, compassion, and emptiness. In other words, the qualities of wisdom and kindness are inherent to the mind. No one and nothing added them. They are like the hue of a lawn. The gardener did not paint the grass green; it naturally grew that way. Thus the mind, in its original and stable state, is clarity and emptiness, what we also call Buddha nature.

We can conclude that we do not succeed in remaining with this essence because we are agitated by the emotional and conceptual occurrences that arise in our minds. Why? The mind falls into the trap of its own functioning. The quality of clarity allows the mind to perceive all things, but we do not have direct access to this dimension. It is obscured by several veils: emotions, karma, habits, and knowledge acquired over time. These different layers of obscuration accumulate on top of our original state over the course of our past and present lives.

The process of apprehending an object triggers various mental occurrences. Once the mind registers the presence of an object (either physical or mental), these adventitious obscurations take over the information and interpret it according to their own criteria, which prevents us from remaining in the natural dimension of our minds. The process of life as we know it thus begins.

The cause that triggers this mechanism lies in the belief in the existence of a self, often translated as "self-clinging." This profound conviction perpetuates itself and then solidifies based on the different experiences we undergo. Self-clinging, or ego-clinging, notably manifests through identification with our bodies, our names, our feelings, and our opinions. It is the habit of identification with ourselves. The simplest example to become aware of it is the example of our names. Our names are so familiar to us that they seems to be part of us, to be ourselves.

Let us consider a concrete example to better understand how this clinging operates. Imagine buying a new car. When we own a brand new car, we are extremely concerned with not damaging it. We take care of not giving it the slightest scratch and we wash it as soon as it is even a little dirty. We become sensitive to all of these precautions immediately upon buying a new car. Furthermore, if we have to park it in an unsafe neighborhood, we constantly worry about it. On the other hand, our experience will be different if we understand that our car is liable to get scratched at any moment and will inevitably be scratched at some point or another, and this is not a crisis. The unpleasant feelings of worry will not overwhelm us in the same way. We will be able to maintain perspective with our anxiety. The same is true of the mind. Understanding and accepting this identification with a self makes us free.

Our excessive attachment governs the emotional and conceptual occurrences of our minds. These occurrences sometimes push us in a beneficial direction and sometimes in a harmful one. Anger, jealousy, pride, desire, fear—just to name a few—and our experience of life in general arise based on this attachment.

Reading or listening to this explanation is not sufficient for it have a concrete effect on our daily lives. We must acquire a personal experience of the teachings. In this case, genuine change occurs naturally. We can acquire this experience through observing our minds and identifying the feelings and other occurrences that emerge, as we have explained in the previous chapters. As long as we have not integrated this explanation, there is no real freedom. The signification of clarity and emptiness is that we no longer experience any identification with a self.

In Buddhism, liberation is not something mystic filled with fantastical experiences. In contrast with this notion, Buddhist liberation is a definitive understanding of the absurdity of this self. When we realize that it is not necessary for this clinging to define us, the way we perceive life completely changes.

## The Nature of Other Phenomena

On the basis of this first understanding, the teachings offer us a little space in our minds and allow our reality to become less solid and fixed. At this point, it is useful to more closely observe the objects of our perception—both material objects and those that arise in the mind. Do they truly have the reality we accord them? The teaching *Placing the Focus Closest to Four [Objects]* shows that external objects, along with our feelings, do not exist as solidly as we tend to believe. What we call a "table" today was a tree yesterday and may be firewood tomorrow. Just like our selves, external phenomena arise from the unification of causes and conditions and are subject to the passage of time.

Furthermore, our partial perception leads us to construct our own versions of things. When we drink water, we only experience our personal version of water, which is not the same as the reality of water. We think that what we perceive truly exists as we experience it, but in truth we project our own concepts on reality.

This realization may seem strange, since our perceptions seem real to us, just as our "I" seems to exist. Continuing to function based on the certainty of our perceptions means solidifying the basis for our unhappiness. Bodhisattvas, on the contrary, adopt a state of mind that is counter to our ordinary functioning. They know that external objects do not have any permanent reality and that the natural state of mind is beyond any categorization. If we integrate this reality, we no longer experience dualistic perception. We no longer function in terms of a person who perceives an object that is truly present. We become free from our fixed personal ideas and our individual versions of reality. We are able to apprehend things as they truly are. Freedom from attachment naturally arises. Because there is less self-identification, the causes for the manifestation of attachment, discontent, and dissatisfaction disappear. We cut off unhappiness at the root. Bodhisattvas live according to this understanding, beyond the typical ideas of human beings.

### Not Giving In

Due to this understanding, a bodhisattva does not suffer from any arrogance, even if he is famous, respected by all, and living in great luxury. He understands that his possessions and his fame are nothing other than conditioned phenomena that are subject to change. Not succumbing to pride protects him from the errors that this sentiment can bring.

Free from rejection or judgment, a bodhisattva perceives phenomena in the same way as a rainbow. We all know that the appearance of a rainbow is a temporary effect of atmospheric conditions. We all appreciate its beauty, but no one is surprised when it disappears. A bodhisattva sees all phenomena in this way, including those that are pleasant and attractive. They manifest, but they have no ultimate reality. He does not give in to the attachment that can develop based on personal preference. Approaching phenomena this way prevents them from being a source of unhappiness for him.

When an object fascinates us, it attracts us and preoccupies our minds. We want to enjoy it as much as possible and to possess it. However, if we change our opinion later on, the same object that seemed essential to us before then becomes unimportant and is no longer capable of fascinating us in the same way. Yet the object itself is the same. Realizing this allows us to see that our own perceptions delude us more than the object itself. We assign a reality to our passing feelings and commit ourselves accordingly.

Understanding this is essential. This functioning does not only apply to insignificant attachments; it is identical for everything that we experience. Though we manage to find solutions for the basic problems of everyday life, this does not resolve the fundamental problems caused by this perpetual process of appropriation. They continue to imprison us and cause us unhappiness.

When we realize that external phenomena function more like the imagery of a dream than a truly solid reality and that our states of mind fluctuate based on the intensity of our grasping, we gain perspective on our own mental discourse. Through this training, we can weaken the hold of our beliefs and opinions on our minds and become more flexible. When this self loses ground, it leaves space for less agitation and greater stability.

On this basis, we can establish a new relationship with attachment and rejection. We will even experience suffering in a different way. A bodhisattva considers the difficulties that he encounters with the same understanding of illusion as he does pleasant things. As he is aware of the genesis of unhappiness, he does not give in to or identify with the appearance of its causes. Suffering is the result of a sequence of emotions and concepts based on attachment to a self. A bodhisattva clearly sees the unreal aspect of this process, which dissipates the rejection of an unpleasant feeling or the attachment to a pleasant one.

A precise understanding of these notions does not occur in the space of a few hours. The objects that surround us, the feelings we experience, and the beliefs to which we hold make up our daily universe. It is only possible to properly question them through profound reflection. If we do not understand this, we risk terminating our investigation upon our very first conclusion.

Furthermore, understanding develops through the process of daily meditation. Meditation allows us to experience a way of knowing beyond words. Without this aspect of practice, the boundaries of intellect and of our beliefs restrict us. We read the different chapters of this book and more or less understand them. The problem, though, lies in these very approximations and this lack of precision, which reinforce confusion.

Meditation based on reflection allows for an understanding that is different than our habitual representations. However, for this clarification to occur, we need a long-term habit of meditation. Then, based on our experience and the instructions, we will eventually realize that each of our individual versions of the world is not an objective reality. We will see that it is the product of our veils, which obscure the nature of mind. Our interpretations of the world arise based on our obscurations, and we take this vision to be reality. Regular meditation practice gives us the opportunity to break free from this unreliable version of reality. Of course, it is important to remember that we cannot force the result. Understanding appears based on our own abilities and rhythm. By practicing with respect to this, our relationships to attachment and rejection change naturally. In addition, practicing in accordance with our own capacities prevents us from falling into the trap of fascination.

In one of the chapters of *The Jewel Ornament of Liberation*, Gampopa explains that bodhisattvas continue to dissolve their obscurations all the way until they become enlightened. Even if we eliminate the most basic obscurations, the most subtle remain. Becoming free from our habitual functioning takes time for all of us.

## Attention and Awareness

Bodhisattvas rely on two indispensable tools to evolve beyond their fundamental habits: attention and awareness. As in meditative training, attention means being present to oneself and awareness implies recognizing the occurrences that arise in the mind. Generally, meditation allows us to train in not letting the mind wander. We acquire the ability to identify the feelings and concepts that are present so that we do not follow them.

A bodhisattva's great experience in this practice allows him to apply it in daily situations. As soon as a feeling or perception appears, he immediately sees it and recognizes its origin.

Emotional and conceptual occurrences naturally and instantaneously arise in the mind. Once they settle in and take root, it is difficult to remedy them. Therefore, the goal is not to let these habits perpetuate themselves. We do so based on a presence of mind that is both attentive and aware.

Consider an example of how to use the tools of attention and awareness. For no apparent reason, we feel discontent. Attention allows us to identify this feeling as soon as it emerges. We then begin to look for the cause of this unhappiness: solitude, boredom, etc. Due to this lucid analysis, we become aware that a specific unsatisfied desire is at the source of this dissatisfaction. We then seek out the source of this desire. Where did it come from? What triggered it? If we follow the thread back, we will arrive at the source: profound attachment, which is in fact self-grasping. Through this observation of the origin of our experience, we can act on the causes of our final discontent.

For this method to be efficient, we must apply it regularly in different contexts until we see that this process permeates all of life. Our difficulties as well as our joys are directly connected with this fundamental attachment. So long as we do not realize that this grasping is unnecessary, our emotions continue to fluctuate in accordance with it. Our states of mind change ceaselessly and cause our various dissatisfactions.

Constantly armed with attention and awareness, a

bodhisattva cuts off habits before they become unmanageable. Whatever the circumstances, he stays fully conscious of his current state of mind. Because he is less emotionally entangled in the situations he encounters, he is more present to others and thus more available for them. At our level, the objective is not to be perfect but rather to clearly see our imperfections in order to act on their causes.

## Dedicating Beneficial Actions

Improving our understanding of the nature of phenomena and of our minds gradually weakens duality's hold over us. Another practice of bodhisattvas leads in this same direction: dedicating beneficial acts, also called merit. This practice consists in dedicating the benefit we and others accomplish to all beings. In the beginning, this means thinking of others according to the perspective of enlightened mind. Creating this habit directs the mind toward others without an expectation of personal gain. In consequence, this leads to a certain freedom from attachment; we offer our best actions for others. In this way, the ego can no longer appropriate them for itself.

Most of the time, we expect a reward for our actions. Whether consciously or unconsciously, we anticipate a response, most often a gesture of gratitude. The perspective of enlightened mind excludes all personal expectations or calculations of "return on investment." For example, the practice of generosity means serving beings without manipulation or ulterior motives. We tend to easily slant things to our own advantage. Enlightened mind proposes another way of being. As we are committing to a gradual path of training, we each begin at our own level in order to evolve toward un-conditional action. Additionally, it is useful to keep in mind that there is no qualitative scale for actions, with certain actions ranking as more beneficial than others. From the moment that the motivation is sincere and the action just, the benefits are identical. Furthermore, ded-icating the benefit of an act for all beings amplifies its value.

This dedication of merit takes on another dimension when carried out by a bodhisattva. In this case, it occurs on the basis of an understanding of the nature of phe-nomena and of mind. The mind is the instrument that allows the dedication of merit. If the mind is not limited or subject to self-attachment, the dedication transcends a simple thought. It truly comes to be and thus com-pletes the beneficial act.

The mind must be constantly vigilant—in the mo-ment that the intention for an act arises, during the accomplishment of the act, and also after, by accompa nying the act through its conclusion by dedicating its benefit. Maintaining a quality of presence throughout these three phases protects us from the influence of ego-clinging and helps us plant the seeds of enlightened attitude.

# A Final Note

The bodhisattva's path is that of kindness and compassion. Thus, it involves committing to beneficial activity and giving up causing harm. The path can help to resolve numerous problems and even lead us to be completely free from unhappiness. Embracing the bodhisattva's attitude begins with an observation of what makes up our reality: our human existence, our minds, our feelings and our actions. The path thus begins with a sincere observation of ourselves in order to perceive our own functioning. Reference points—the Buddha, his methods, and our traveling companions—offer support and act as landmarks on the path.

A beginner does not need any particular environment in order to apply their advice. He can simply use the circumstances that manifest around him—daily life. Forcing progress does not give lasting results. Only personal understanding and integration give rise to stable progress. Application must be in accordance with our own capacities. There is no point in being overly demanding. Instead, we begin by noticing an attitude, a feeling, or a form of agitation. And we try to discover what is happening within ourselves by following the proposed method. On this basis, we can then conduct experiments in not following the occurrences that we identify. This iterative method emphasizes the process over the final result, as the process itself determines the result.

The practice of meditation is another important element in the evolution toward the bodhisattva's attitude. It brings us two things. First, it allows us to gain greater clarity of mind and thus better understanding. Second, it allows us to digest information and experiences through a means other than the intellect. Meditation practice facilitates the integration and adoption of the ideas of the Buddhist teachings and helps us personally understand them. It is important to understand the necessity of regular training in meditation. Over time, the clarity we acquire dissipates confusion and offers a better understanding of what happens in the mind as well as in the situations we encounter in daily life.

This book is based on the Buddha's teaching. Anyone who truly wishes to commit to the path of enlightened mind must take the time to learn the values and qualities of the Buddha, his methods, and those who have applied and fully accomplished them. This step is crucial, for it allows us develop confidence in the teachings and the result. This confidence serves as a reference point throughout our progress on the path, even in the face of doubts. Without this confidence, we have difficulty persevering and being patient. We risk choosing to follow our own interpretations, which will not lead us to the result we initially sought.

Understanding what a Buddha is requires profound training in the teachings. We cannot develop confidence based on personal preference; it is not a question of liking the Buddha but of understanding what makes such a being utterly extraordinary. What is this freedom that he discovered? If we wish to become Buddhas ourselves, it is essential that we understand the meaning of these ideas.

It is possible to partially apply oneself to the bodhisattva's path. As explained, this offers non-negligible relative results such as greater calm and an improved approach to difficulties, etc. However, if these accomplishments do not constitute our final goal, we must take care not to get stuck at this level. To ensure good progress toward enlightenment, a practitioner needs to train in three practices: study of the teachings (which also includes contemplation), meditation, and beneficial action or service for others. We must bring together all three elements in order to achieve the result. One or two aspects will not suffice; leaving out elements can lead us in an extreme direction that will prevent us from attaining our goal.

The practice of meditation alone, without knowledge of the teachings, does indeed develop clarity of mind. However, there is no guarantee that the orientation of this clarity will allow us to realize the qualities of a bodhisattva.

If we concentrate our efforts solely on studying the teachings, we will become great scholars capable of impressive speeches, but we will not evolve because we will not know how to apply our knowledge in practical situations.

Lastly, if we do not integrate study and meditation into daily activity, it is not possible to acquire personal and concrete experience of the teachings. In complement, beneficial action generates positive potential, also called merit. This merit functions like a reserve of energy for pursuing the path, similar to putting gas in a car.

There is no miracle here. Combining these three elements demands effort. The work begins with small things in daily life. Try to study and meditate a little each day and to consider situations through the lens of the Buddha's teaching. Try being helpful without any expectation for a particular sentiment or gain in return, while simply rejoicing in the benefit for ourselves and others. Progress comes through applying these three aspects continuously, without forcing, but while simply keeping the mind relaxed.

As practitioners, when we decide to follow this path, we must make a commitment—one that is both firm and flexible. On first glance, these terms may seem contradictory. "Firm" means that even if we get discouraged, we will not abandon our commitment, but continue what we have set out to do. However, to avoid rigidity, we must keep our commitment flexible. Indeed, perfectly maintaining our commitment is nearly impossible. We will make mistakes. However, by correcting them, we progress. In addition, flexibility gives us the opportunity to adjust our efforts according to our current capacities without falling into complacency.

The basic commitment of a bodhisattva instructs us not to cause harm and instead to be useful to others. Thus, the idea is to remain firm and not abandon this goal. We do our best as human beings, though it is very difficult not to cause harm. Flexibility allows us to commit to this path. Without it, we would be incapable of taking a single step in this direction because, as we know, perfection is practically impossible. With both this flexibility and steadfastness, we can make mistakes, learn from them, and continue.

One of the fundamental ideas of the Buddha's teaching is that of bringing peace and harmony. Yet, if our own minds are not at peace, how can we be agents for harmony around ourselves? We can sign peace treaties, shake hands, and agree that everything is alright, but this does not last. Disputes and conflicts quickly arise again because this type of peace is only artificial. We cannot force peace. Peace is the expression of understanding—the understanding of our minds' functioning. Once we have achieved this, nothing more can trouble our minds. In Buddhism, peace and harmony do not refer to a calm and quiet place where everyone is serene. Instead, peace and harmony refer to a mind that maintains its own stability, regardless of the situations it encounters. As we move forward, let us keep this in mind and remember that the goal of the bodhisattva's path is to diminish unhappiness.

Publishing finished
in June 2019 by Pulsio
Publisher Number : 0023
Legal Deposit : October 2016
Printed in Bulgaria